A H I K E R ' S G U I D E

T O A R T O F T H E C A N A D I A N

R O C K I E S

Cover: Detail of *Sage Brush,* undated,
by Carl Rungius, oil on canvas, Glenbow
Collection
Inset: Walter J. Phillips at work,
Bow Summit, 1936

Published by:
Glenbow Museum
130–9th Avenue S.E.,
Calgary, Alberta, Canada T2G 0P3
E-mail: Glenbow @ lexicom.ab.ca
Web site: http://www.lexicom.ab.ca/~glenbow

Printed in Canada by Sundog Printing Limited,
on recycled paper.

Editor: Donna Livingstone
Design: Cathie Ross
Photography: Anita Dammer

Canadian Cataloguing in
Publication Data

Christensen, Lisa
A hiker's guide to art of the Canadian
Rockies

Includes bibliographical references and
index.
ISBN 1-895379-44-X

   1. Hiking–Rocky Mountains, Canadian
(B.C. and Alta.) –Guidebooks. 2. Rocky
Mountains, Canadian (B.C. and Alta.)
–Guidebooks. 3. Rocky Mountains,
Canadian (B.C. and Alta.) in art.
I Title

GV199.44C22R64 1996   917.1104'4

C96-900470-2

A Hiker's Guide
To Art Of The Canadian
Rockies

Lisa Christensen

TO MY FATHER, WHO TAUGHT ME TO LOVE THE MOUNTAINS,

TO MY MOTHER, WHO TALKED ABOUT WATERCOLOURS,

AND TO DAVID, WHO ENCOURAGED ME.

Frederick Brigden
Bow Lake, undated
watercolour on paper, Glenbow Collection

Thanks must go first and foremost to Donna Livingstone, for her never-ending patience, willingness to give her time, and boundless excitement for the project. To the staff of Glenbow, who supported the project and helped to make it happen, and who have allowed me the freedom to work in an unconventional way. To Jeanne Watson for her careful edits, Cathie Ross for her creative design and innovative ideas, and Anita Dammer for her painstaking photographs. Also thanks to Mary Lender for dealing with millions of details, and Lindsay Moir for preparing the index. To all those who agreed from the start that there are more ways to appreciate art than just in a gallery, thanks for your support.

To the staff in the collections, registration departments, libraries, and archives of the McMichael Canadian Art Collection, the National Gallery of Canada, the University of British Columbia Fine Arts Collection, the Whyte Museum of the Canadian Rockies, the Art Gallery of Ontario, the Vancouver Art Gallery, The Edmonton Art Gallery, the Art Gallery of Hamilton, the Montreal Museum of Fine Arts, the London Regional Art and Historical Museums, the Fogg Art Museum, Harvard University, and the National Archives of Canada, who answered questions, shared research, met impossible deadlines, and brought out file after file. To these and to the many public and private collectors, individuals, and corporations that have permitted the use of their works, I extend sincere thanks.

Thanks are due to Sepp Renner at Mount Assiniboine Lodge, who pointed out specific places, named them accurately, and tried to teach me how to make telemark turns in eight feet of fresh snow; to Blake O'Brien at Skoki Mountain Lodge, who helped me figure out the perspective of A.C. Leighton's Skoki paintings; to the staff of Maligne Lake Tours, who permitted lengthy stopovers at Spirit Island.

To the mountain writers and photographers, Scott Rowed, Brian Patton, Don Beers, Graeme Pole, and others, whose images pointed me down this trail or to that ridge, helped to orient me when north seemed to be south, and Assiniboine just didn't look like Assiniboine, I looked at your photographs hundreds of times.

Christopher Jackson, good friend and formerly senior curator of art at Glenbow, Charles C. Hill, curator of Canadian art at the National Gallery of Canada, and Cathy Mastin, senior curator of art at Glenbow, read the manuscript and provided thoughtful and helpful comments and corrections.

Brian Patton, mountain researcher and author of several publications on the Canadian Rockies, also read the manuscript and verified trail information and provided valuable suggestions on format.

Funding for the publication of this book has been generously provided by The City of Calgary, and the Minister Responsible for Alberta Lotteries and the Department of Community Development of the Province of Alberta. Thanks are due also to The Alberta Museums Association, which provided funding for research.

To my family and friends, many of whom are avid hikers and art lovers, who were interested in where, and when, and who, and kept asking "How's the book coming?" Especially to Nancy, who first told me to "write that down" one summer afternoon in Jasper. To Liz, who endured the deluge at Mount Robson, and had better snacks for the trail than anyone I have ever hiked with. To Cathie and Anita, for their endless patience and constant friendship. To Diane and Roger, Barbara and Don, Linda, Michelle, Dayna, Sues, and Angela, who baby-sat. And to David, who kept telling me that this topic was interesting when I thought I was the only person in the world who wanted to hike to the sites of paintings, for hiking the trails with me, carrying my lap-top computer around Lake O'Hara, making space in his pack for my slides and photographs, and for his constant support and enthusiasm.

J.E.H. MacDonald sketching near Lake O'Hara, c.1924-30

"ART IS THE SUCCESSFUL COMMUNICATION OF A VALUABLE EXPERIENCE."

– J.E.H. MacDonald, 1929

INTRODUCTION 2

HOW TO USE THIS BOOK 6

**CANMORE AND BANFF
NATIONAL PARK** 8
Canmore and Banff Townsites 10
   Ice and Still Water, Canmore 10
   Spring Reflections, Mount Rundle 12
   Mount Rundle, Banff 14
The Bow Valley Parkway 17
   Mountain Road 17
Lake Louise and Area 19
   Rising Clouds, Lake Louise 19
   Morning, Lake Louise 23
   After September Snow, Lake Louise 23
   Lake in the Clouds, Lake Agnes 25
   Mount Lefroy 29
Moraine Lake and Area 30
   Moraine Lake 30
   The Glacier 34
   From Larch Valley, Moraine Lake 37
   On the Rockpile, Looking West,
   Wenkchemna 39
   Mount Fairview from Mount Temple 40
The Trans-Canada Highway 43
   Mount Temple 43
   Castle Mountain 45
Skoki 47
   Ptarmigan Pass, Canadian Rockies 47
   Boulder Pass 49
   Mount Skoki 51
   Brachiopod Mountain 54
   Ptarmigan Peak 54

**MOUNT ASSINIBOINE
PROVINCIAL PARK** 56
   Mount Assiniboine 59
   Mount Assiniboine,
   September Snow 61

YOHO NATIONAL PARK 64
Lake O'Hara 67
   Lake O'Hara, September, 1916 67
   Mount Lefroy, Lake O'Hara 69

   Cathedral Peak and Lake O'Hara 71
   Wiwaxy Peaks, Lake O'Hara 73
   Lake O'Hara with Snow 76
   Lake McArthur, Yoho Park 81
   Cathedral Mountain 85
The Yoho Valley 87
   Clearing Weather, Sherbrooke Lake,
   Above Wapta Lake 87
   Glaciers, Rocky Mountains 89
Emerald Lake 93
   Emerald Lake 93

KOOTENAY NATIONAL PARK 94
   Floe Lake, Marble Canyon 96

THE ICEFIELDS PARKWAY 98
   Crowfoot Glacier 100
   Bow Lake 105
   Mount Athabasca 107

JASPER NATIONAL PARK 108
Maligne Lake 110
   Maligne Lake 110
   Mount Sampson, Maligne Lake 113
The Tonquin Valley 115
   Ramparts, Amethyst Lake,
   Tonquin Valley, Jasper 115

**MOUNT ROBSON PROVINCIAL
PARK** 116
   Mount Robson, Resplendent and Kain 119
   Mount Robson 120
   Tumbling Glacier, Berg Lake 123

CONCLUSION 124

APPENDIX
List of Art and Artists 126
Selected Bibliography 128
Index 130
List of Collectors and Photography Credits 132
Endnotes 133
Suggested Reading 134
Map inset pocket, inside back cover

A.C. Leighton at work, date unknown

"THE FIRST AND MOST IMPORTANT THING IN LANDSCAPE PAINTING

IS TO FIND A NICE COMFORTABLE PLACE TO SIT."

– John William Beatty to A.C. Leighton, 1927

"THE HISTORY OF LANDSCAPE IS THE HISTORY OF THE HUMAN SPIRIT. IT IS CONCERNED WITH ENVIRONMENT — IT IS THE BACKGROUND, THE FOREGROUND, THE MIDDLE DISTANCE, AND THE DISTANCE. IT CONTAINS FLOWERS AND LEAVES, STREAMS AND MOUNTAINS, HILLS AND SKIES. IT IS CONCERNED WITH DETAIL, WITH SPACE, WITH LINE — WITH BEAUTY OF SKY AND THE FIRM AND BOUNTIFUL EARTH, THE EXPANSE AND WONDER OF THE SEA. IT EXPRESSES MOOD, CHARACTER, POETRY, DRAMA — THE GENTLE AND THE SAVAGE, THE PRIMITIVE AND THE SOPHISTICATED. IT IS THE HOME OF LIGHT AND AIR — IT SOFTENS OUR ARROGANCE AND SUPREMACY, SOOTHES OUR LONGINGS AND FRUSTRATIONS."

— Arthur Lismer, lecture notes, undated

For over a century, the scenery of the Canadian Rocky Mountains has romanced travellers and artists alike. People have journeyed great distances to see these mountains, endured physical hardship and sometimes the loss of life while exploring them, and abandoned urban living to be constantly near them. They are an awe inspiring mountain range. From the United States border, they break onto the horizon like a thousand pyramids following a tangled line running northwest to the British Columbia/Yukon border. They are vast and ever-changing, dominating and compelling, a panorama of stone. It is not surprising that the first non-aboriginal artists to depict the Rockies in the 1850s chose to do so in European-influenced Romantic style. They came to the mountains from Europe and the United States, steeped in the poetry of William Wordsworth, the landscape painting of artists such as John Constable and William Turner, and the writings of Henry David Thoreau. Looking at the scenery of Canada through eyes influenced by these traditions, they depicted the land as sublime, magnificent, and glorious.

The human figure is depicted very small in the landscape and has remained so for the last 100 years.

John Hammond's *The Three Sisters* (opposite), exemplifies this artistic preoccupation with notions of Romanticism. The canvas, which hung in the Palliser Hotel in Calgary for many years, conveys a feeling of tremendous space, with the picturesque mountains bathed in a divine light. The tiny plume of smoke, the only evidence of a human element in the work, is minute yet significant, illustrating the perennial tension between man and nature.

The building of the Canadian railway systems in the late nineteenth and early twentieth centuries opened the West to comparatively easy travel. The Canadian Pacific Railway (CPR), and the Canadian Northern Railway (CNR), took artists and other travellers to scenery largely unknown to the world. The potential of the western Canadian Rockies was quickly capitalized upon, particularly by the CPR. A group of artists now known as CPR artists, were among the first groups of trained artists to focus their attention

John Hammond
The Three Sisters, after 1890
oil on canvas, Glenbow Collection

on the Rockies, and their work did much to stimulate an interest in the western landscape. Their images of the magnificent peaks became the West's want ad, calling for tourists, settlers, adventurers, the sick, and the well; offering leisure, recuperation, work, challenges, escape, and opportunity.

As the West was increasingly settled, artists began to establish permanent residences to work, teach, and paint. Colleges were built, art galleries began to open, and a developing sense of nationhood grew throughout the country as the people sought to establish their identity. Colonials became Canadians, and Canadian artists set out to depict the land with a fresh, unique style, responsive to their environment.

In the 1920s, vibrant work by the Group of Seven and their contemporaries challenged the established notion of art-making and called for people of this country to look to their own land and find within it a Canadian art. Their work sparked a nation-wide debate that for many artists inspired a new artistic nationalism. In pursuit of this nationalism, several of the original members of the Group of Seven, including Arthur Lismer, James Edward Hervey (J.E.H.) MacDonald, Lawren Harris,[1] and Alexander Young (A.Y.) Jackson came west to the mountains to paint.[2] Across Canada, art clubs and societies began to actively promote locally-schooled artists, initiating exhibiting programs and generating travelling shows. Much of this art was landscape, and in the West, the Rockies provided ample subject matter.

The artwork that depicts the Canadian Rockies is so bountiful and varied that a comprehensive listing of it, from the earliest watercolours and engravings of the nineteenth century to the works of the present, would fill volumes of trail guides. Virtually every wind-swept valley, seemingly impenetrable glacier, clear mountain lake, larch-filled thicket, and snow-capped peak in the Canadian Rockies has been the subject for paint, print, or pencil, at the hand of an artist. The works discussed in this volume represent a particular period in the art history of the Rockies, from the 1920s to the 1940s, with a few exceptions on either side. The selection also represents the most historically popular sketching destinations in the Rockies; scenes of Lake Louise and Lake O'Hara, for example, are numerous. This reflects the area's long history of having

trails, lodges, and established pack routes, which gave artists easy access to, and comfortable accommodations near, the scenery.

Every visitor approaching the Rockies, whether on a day's ski trip, gazing out the window of a car or bus, or loaded with supplies for a week's trek into the back-country, enters into a relationship with the mountains. These relationships take many forms; romance and wonder, fascination and awe, challenge and the urge to conquer, fear and insignificance, even indifference and disinterest. Each artist, too, depicting the mountains, entered into such a relationship, and through their varied works, we are offered visual insight into our enduring fascination with the peaks, and an opportunity to indulge in our own romance with the Rockies.

"I AM ASKED SOMETIMES HOW TO LOOK AT NATURE; BECAUSE I AM A LANDSCAPE PAINTER

IT IS THOUGHT THAT I MUST HAVE A SURE-FIRE ANSWER. I AM NOT SURE.

I MAY HAVE A KEENER PERCEPTION OF MY OWN BRAND OF BEAUTY SINCE IT IS MY BUSINESS

TO SMELL IT OUT AND REPRODUCE IT, BUT DO I GET MORE PLEASURE OUT OF

SIMPLE CONTEMPLATION OF NATURE? I DON'T DOUBT THAT I DO. SOME OF US ARE ALMOST

PAGAN IN THAT OUR LOVE OF NATURE PREVAILS OVER OUR LOVE OF ART.

THE ARTIST IS SUPPOSED TO LOOK ON LANDSCAPE WITH A PREDATORY EYE, MINDFUL OF

WHAT MAY BE APPROPRIATED THEREFROM. AS THE UNDERTAKER MEASURES THE

CORPSE FOR ITS BOX, SO THE PAINTER MEASURES THE SCENERY…

VISUALIZING ITS ULTIMATE APOTHEOSIS WITHIN A FRAME OF GILT."

— Walter Phillips in *Phillips in Print*, 1940

This book offers readers a chance to follow the steps of artists into the mountains. Beginning with Canmore and Banff, hikers can visit the sites of artworks depicting the massive peaks of The Three Sisters as captured in oil by Illingworth Kerr, the serenity of Walter Phillips's Mount Rundle, or the Skoki region captured in A.C. Leighton's soft watercolours. Lake Louise, Moraine Lake, and the adjacent valley systems are represented by the paintings of Belmore Browne, Peter and Catharine Whyte, and Carl Rungius. The Yoho Valley and the environs of Lake O'Hara are explored primarily through the work of J.E.H. MacDonald, who painted in the area for seven consecutive years, until his death. Mount Assiniboine Provincial Park, Mount Robson Provincial Park, and Jasper National Park, including Maligne Lake, were painted by members of the Group of Seven who came west to paint.

A number of the artworks are winter scenes, and to fully appreciate the conditions that would have existed when the artists were working, cross-country skiing is in order. As well, a number of works depicting places along the Trans-Canada Highway, the Bow Valley Parkway, and the Icefields Parkway, by a variety of artists and at varying times of year, are included for those days when you are travelling by car.

The hikes listed in this book are intended to take you to the places that are depicted in each artwork. In most instances, exact directions to specific locations are given. In some cases, however, trails do not exist; they have been re-routed, no longer exist, or are permanently closed. Directions that follow current trails and reach the best possible approximations of the artist's composition are listed for such sites. Works which have titles that make the location clearly obvious are not accompanied by detailed trail information.

Please consult one of the many excellent hiking guides available for full trail information on each location, in particular for backcountry and overnight hikes. A list of suggested reading has been included for your reference. Backcountry camping permits are required and enforced in many places, and trail quotas, campfire restrictions, and registration procedures are becoming common in the Rockies. Contact the pertinent national or provincial park office before you go to be certain of what you can expect on the trail.

Hikers should remain on the established trails to avoid causing environmental damage. Appropriate clothing and footwear are essential for hiking in the mountains, and should never be left behind, even on a short hike in pleasant weather. Trails become slippery with only a few flakes of snow, and snow falls every month of the year in the Rockies. Whenever you are in the mountains, be aware of safety and environmental factors such as trail erosion and sensitive landscapes, wildlife (especially elk and bears), and the unpredictable temper of the weather.

A number of discrepancies exist in the geographical place-names where they have been used as titles of some of the artworks. In several cases, there is a minor spelling difference between the given title and the place-name; others are more confusing. These have been addressed in the text.

Some artworks were completed on the spot, others were worked up in the artist's studio from sketches, and are referred to as studio works.

Trail information is provided in the sidebar format.

Note: For roadside sites, some trail information will not apply.

Catharine Robb Whyte and hiking companions, c.1930

TRAIL INFO

Trail/site information: The location of the scene depicted in the art denoted by trail or region place-name, or the site depicted in the work if a roadside view

Type of hike: Half-day or day hike, backcountry overnight hike, climb, or roadside view

Best time to go: To see the light, atmospheric, and seasonal conditions that echo those depicted in the artwork

Trailhead: Parking and location of the start of the trail

Distance: Hiking distance in kilometres one way

Elevation gain: From trailhead to highest point on the trail

Degree of difficulty: Very easy, easy, moderate, difficult, very difficult

Hiking/viewing time: Approximate total hiking time from the trailhead to the site in the artwork and return. Viewing time denotes roadside sites.

Driving time (roadside sites): Approximate time to drive the road along which the subject of the artwork appears, from the nearest town or city

Topo map(s): Canadian Department of Energy, Mines and Resources topographical map reference numbers

Route: Describes in very basic terms, the topography and nature of the trail; lists switchbacks, junctions, orientation points, viewpoints, and the best places to view the scene of the artwork.

"COLOUR, LIKE MUSIC, IS A UNIVERSAL LANGUAGE

THAT WARMS THE SOUL."

— Illingworth Kerr in *Paint and Circumstance*, 1987

Illingworth Kerr
Ice and Still Water, Canmore, 1969
oil on canvas, Glenbow Collection

CANMORE AND BANFF TOWNSITES

ICE AND STILL WATER, CANMORE

Situated at the eastern gateway to Banff National Park, the charming mountain community of Canmore rests against the foot of the mountain triplets known as The Three Sisters. These distinctive, massive peaks are a familiar beacon to many locals, and are visible for several miles along the Trans-Canada Highway that runs past Canmore. They lead you up into Alberta's Kananaskis Country and back down into the Bow Valley. Although Canmore is a peaceful respite from the busy flurry of Banff and her tourists, it is also developing rapidly. When Illingworth Kerr captured the staunch, reposing sisterhood of these peaks in 1969, the homes and buildings that you will now see when you visit Canmore, did not protrude into the edges of his composition.

Kerr was born in Lumsden, Saskatchewan, and studied at the Ontario College of Art under Arthur Lismer, J.E.H. MacDonald, Frederick Varley, and J.W. Beatty, all important artists whose teachings influenced Kerr. He learned to see and to depict colour and light from Arthur Lismer, who told him to "Look for the prismatic light changes in skies,"[3] and developed a feel for the quality of his painted surfaces by repeated practice. He studied the composition of clouds, and learned that each type of atmospheric formation affected how he would apply colour when painting them. Through these teachers and his own inquiries, Kerr came to be able to depict light and colour in landscape in a fresh and unique way, with a patience for the less picturesque moments, and an eye for the spectacular ones:

"Nature does not always afford a perfect example, but sometimes the horizon shimmers in yellowish viridian, moves up to cobalt, then up to zenith in ultramarine. Similarly the clouds begin low down in pink with blue shadows and climb through orange and change until glowing with yellow light."[4]

As a student, Kerr was somewhat of an idealist, with dreams of making art, being inspired, and simply creating; however, he gradually came to understand the realities of a career in painting. Beatty's advice that "The first and most important thing in landscape painting is to find a nice comfortable place to sit" only "insulted and flabbergasted" Kerr. "I wanted inspiration, not convenience," he later said. "But the truth is that many studies are ruined or never completed through discomfort."[5]

Kerr's confident brushwork captures the regular, geometric formations of The Three Sisters in sharply cut, gemstone geometry, which emphasizes the angular solidity of their forms. It is a still fall day, with low, yellow-grey skies that speak of snow. The peaks are reflected in the remarkably still water showing depth and clarity where the ice has not yet finished creeping across its surface. The atmosphere in the work is tangible, and Kerr's ability to render light effects shows clearly.

Ice and Still Water, Canmore, was painted relatively late in Kerr's career, after his retirement from a dedicated and influential life of teaching, first in Vancouver, then in Calgary, where he directed the art school of the Provincial Institute of Technology and Art (now the Alberta College of Art and Design, or ACAD) from 1947 to 1967. These years were "a time of rebirth"[6] in Alberta; relieved from the struggles of the Depression and the war, the province was prospering under a government reaping financial rewards from the newly discovered Leduc oil fields.

After Kerr's retirement from ACAD, he devoted himself to full-time painting and secured a number of important portrait commissions. He also took several painting trips to eastern Canada, and was able to look at a wide variety of art while there, including works by members of the Group of Seven. Viewing their tangled landscapes served only to further cultivate his love of the flat, serene landscapes of the Saskatchewan and Alberta prairie. Largely overlooked by members of the Group of Seven,[7] the prairies, with their endless horizons, dramatic light effects, subtle colour, and vast serenity, became his focus and his true landscape.

TRAIL INFO

Trail information:
The Three Sisters
Type of hike: Roadside view
Best time to go: Very early morning in the fall when the ice is just beginning to form on the edges of the river
Viewing time: Allow 15 minutes to view the site of the work from the roadside, longer if you intend to walk along the riverbank
Route: Unfortunately, there is no convenient pull-out on the Trans-Canada Highway from which to view The Three Sisters. Instead, you should park in the Town of Canmore and walk along the Bow River pathway on the east bank of the river from the centre of Canmore townsite to the southern edges of town, a distance of less than 10 city blocks. The best approximation in Canmore of Kerr's composition is found at the point where the pathway passes near the corner of 8th Avenue and 3rd Street. A conveniently placed bench looks over the river towards the peaks. Enjoy the scene from there.

Belmore Browne
Spring Reflections (Mount Rundle), undated
oil on canvas, Glenbow Collection

"A PAINTER OF LANDSCAPE INTERPRETS HIS OWN PERSONALITY QUITE AS ADEQUATELY AS THAT OF THE COUNTRY HE PLACES ON CANVAS. WERE IT OTHERWISE, PICTURES OF THE SAME SUBJECT MADE BY VARIOUS ARTISTS WOULD SEEM HOPELESSLY MONOTONOUS."

— Anonymous exhibition leaflet, The Casson Galleries, undated

SPRING REFLECTIONS, MOUNT RUNDLE

As well-known to locals and as predominate on the skyline as The Three Sisters peaks, is the rounded, undulating, up-thrust edge of Mount Rundle. The mountain is within easy walking distance of Banff townsite, and is a relatively low, spreading mountain. It is actually termed a massif (a group of individual peaks running in a band) and is visible from many places along the nearby Bow River and Vermilion Lakes. Although Vermilion Lakes Drive is by far the best place for classic views of Mount Rundle, the Lake Minnewanka Loop Drive, the meadows east of Banff, and the general northeastern vicinity of Banff townsite allow different and interesting vantages. Screened through a grove of poplars, clear and sharp against the sky, or capped with clouds and hanging with snow, the distinctive uppermost edge of this peak is easily recognizable, and from many of the foregoing vantage points, it is reflected in the waters of the Bow River or Vermilion Lakes.

Belmore Browne represents a generation of resident artists who painted the Rockies. In his youth, before he lived in Canada, Browne's family had taken a trip up the west coast of Canada and visited Alaska. This trip had a dramatic impact on Browne, and he developed a love for the wild. Soon after, the Browne family settled in the Pacific Northwest where Browne grew up in a largely rural setting, fostering his love of nature and the outdoors, and becoming wilderness hardy. He attended the New York School of Art and the Académie Julian in Paris.

He then renewed his love for Alaska by joining expeditions to the North, working as an artist, hunter, and specimen preparer for the American Museum of Natural History. During these expeditions, he climbed Mount McKinley twice. He became a noted authority on the North, publishing books and articles and giving lectures. His love for the outdoors drew him to settle in Banff in 1921, where he spent the next 19 years exploring and painting, becoming an outspoken advocate of wilderness preservation, and providing guidance and advice to younger artists.

From his home in Banff, Browne extensively explored the nearby areas on foot, particularly in winter, and came to know the mountains intimately. He was a patient artist, waiting for the perfect light and weather conditions to set the stage for the perfect scene. His work shows a deep understanding of nature and the mountain environment through precise depictions of atmospheric effects. He studied the same places, painting them at various times of year in different conditions, growing to understand their subtle nuances more and more with each painting.

Spring Reflections (Mount Rundle) conveys with sharp accuracy the sense of a cold spring day in the mountains. The scene in the painting is composed from near the second Vermilion Lake, looking southeast. Browne has caught Mount Rundle in heavy snow, and would have had to deal with all the difficulties of freezing paints, frozen feet, and the general chill that comes with a sedentary activity such as painting outdoors in winter. Still, he has taken time to fully observe all the signs of spring that appear in the picture — the dried stalks of grass newly uncovered from the winter snow, the receding ice on the lake melting in that characteristic way that spring ice has, the water stirring with the life of a spring breeze. Hints of new green contrast with the blue-whites of heavy, wet snow covering Rundle and the mountains beyond, and are reflected in the pale mauve waters of the lake.

Walter J. Phillips
Mount Rundle, Banff, 1945
watercolour on paper, Glenbow Collection

"[MOUNT RUNDLE IS MY] 'BREAD AND BUTTER MOUNTAIN'. I NEVER TIRE OF PAINTING IT, FOR IT IS NEVER THE SAME. IN DEEP SHADOW IN THE MORNING, IT BORROWS A WARM GLOW FROM THE SETTING SUN AT THE END OF THE DAY. ITS COLOUR RUNS THE GAMUT FROM ORANGE TO COLD BLUE-GREY, WITH OVERTONES OF VIOLET AND INTERVALS OF GREEN."

— Walter Phillips in *Wet Paint*, c.1940s

MOUNT RUNDLE, BANFF

British-born artist Walter Phillips had already exhibited as a watercolourist with the British Royal Academy by the time he immigrated to Canada in 1913. He settled in Winnipeg, where he became an art instructor at St. John's Technical High School, remaining there until 1924. After a brief return to England, he settled permanently in Canada where he lived in Winnipeg, Calgary, and Banff. He later retired to Victoria where he died in 1963.

Phillips was a master printmaker, and also a skilled etcher. Etching required that Phillips's drawing skills be exacting and sure, and evidence of his accuracy, precise mark-making ability, and sureness of hand, is clear in all of his work. But etching did not allow him to explore colour, and from it, Phillips turned to the colour woodcut. This, along with watercolour, were the media in which he would excel, and the media that would bring him international acclaim. From master Japanese printmaker Yoshiburo Urushibara, Phillips learned a particular method of sizing handmade Japanese paper that enabled him to produce incredibly fine gradations of colour and smooth, silk-like print surfaces.

Phillips was living in Winnipeg when he first had an opportunity to visit the Rockies in 1926. With fellow artists Eric Bergman and Tom MacLean, he set out for Lake O'Hara, the destination of choice for so many artists planning their first sketching trip to the Rockies. The three artists had high hopes for long, clear sketching days, and although they started in good weather, were to spend the bulk of their trip in the rain:

"We decided to camp, and looked forward to an uninterrupted orgy of sketching, carefree, comfortably untidy, paint-slinging furiously from dawn to dewy eve. The reality proved very different… Mountains are always changing. One artist may respond to the effect of brilliant sunshine in clear weather; another may see beauty in the vari-hued strata of which the earth's crust is composed, and produce mountainsides resembling a cut of streaky bacon, while a third prefers the soft effects of rain, smoke or mist… We had no choice; we automatically became artists of the third class. We rarely saw the sun, and bacon dominated our diet so completely that we felt we were under no obligation to paint it too."[8]

Phillips made several trips west to paint the Rockies,

and in the summer of 1940, was invited to teach at the Banff School of Fine Arts, now The Banff Centre for Continuing Education. In the fall of the following year, the Provincial Institute of Technology and Art (Tech) also offered him a teaching position, and Phillips moved to Calgary to manage both positions. The change from Winnipeg, where he had been living and sketching for 25 years, was easily made, due in part to the vast new sketching grounds that beckoned so close at hand.

Phillips would teach at the Banff School of Fine Arts for 20 years, and work out of the school as an unofficial artist-in-residence. In 1946 he built a home in Banff, on the Tunnel Mountain road overlooking the Bow Valley. This would be his base for the next 14 years, where, in close proximity to his favourite sketching haunts, he began to work extensively in the mountains, sketching at high and low elevations, and under all sorts of conditions:

"I like to sketch the year round, in summer when conditions are most comfortable, as well as in winter when one is liable to freeze to death. Each season has its charm, and gives way to the next before one's visual digestion is ruined by repletion… Coloured chalks, pastels, charcoal and pencil, aren't affected by the cold and may be used instead of watercolour, for as long as the sketcher continues immune also. At thirty or forty degrees below zero, the fingers stiffen very quickly without protection. Woollen gloves are clumsy but permit the use of a pencil, but a sock is the best protection of all. It is pulled over the hand and the pencil point thrust through the toe. The fingers thus have full play and will keep warm, provided the sock is thick enough. The number of lines drawn depends upon the temperature…."[9]

Phillips saw "Beauty everywhere — austere and noble on the higher levels, pretty in the valleys …,"[10] and found ways around the less paintable areas of the Rockies that frustrated the less adventurous sketcher who would not leave the security of main roads and trailways:

"The lower slopes of the surrounding mountains, are well-covered with lodgepole pine… Willows and poplars grow in the valley too, and Douglas firs dot the slopes. But all have green leaves; the shrubs and grass beneath them are green, and the reeds under the river banks and on the lakes afford no relief to the eye…the pervading green in a summer landscape is generally oppressive to the spirit of the artist. He looks for relief to the heights above the trees, the region of bare rocks, water, snow, and ice. These heights can be easily reached; and, be it said, only in the mountains can he paint snow pictures comfortably in his shirt sleeves."[11]

TRAIL INFO

Trail information: Mount Rundle from Vermilion Lakes Drive
Type of hike: Roadside view
Best time to go: Early spring, after a fresh snowfall
Distance: 4.8 km
Driving time: Allow 45 minutes; more time if you want to park and explore on foot
Route: Vermilion Lakes Drive is marked with a sign just before Banff's west exit road reaches the Trans-Canada overpass below Mount Norquay. This pleasant and picturesque road provides excellent viewpoints for observing Mount Rundle. The Vermilion Lakes, called first, second, and third, are actually marshes on the Bow River flood plain. The second Vermilion Lake is the best place to stop. If you pull over next to the boat launch, you can enjoy the classic view of Mount Rundle. Water in parts of these marshes stays open all year round, so you can also approximate the scene in the dead of winter if you are out skiing.

Walter J. Phillips
Mountain Road, 1942
colour woodcut on paper, Glenbow Collection

"THE ART OF PRINTMAKING IS A DISTINCT

RESPONSIBILITY. A POOR PAINTING MAY BE A CRIME,

BUT ONLY ONE: A POOR PRINT IS A CRIME

MULTIPLIED BY THE SIZE OF THE EDITION."

— Walter Phillips in *Phillips in Print*, c.1945

THE BOW VALLEY PARKWAY

MOUNTAIN ROAD

Peaceful Highway 1A, known as the Bow Valley Parkway, is a winding, two-lane road that runs roughly parallel to the Trans-Canada Highway for 50 kilometres, from just west of Banff townsite to below the Lake Louise Ski Area. In peak traffic times it is busy, but during the rest of the year is lonely compared to the Trans-Canada Highway. By bicycle or car, the road is worth taking to enjoy the closeness of the forest, the greater likelihood of spotting wildlife, and the numerous lookouts and points of interest, including spectacular Johnston Canyon, along the way.

Walter Phillips delighted in the patterns he observed in the details of nature, including the action of water coursing over rocks, reflections of light and shadow in still pools, and the varied colours of light on the surface of snow. This delicate image, depicting a brilliant sunlit winter day, exemplifies his writings on this subject:

"The problem of painting snow is of colour rather than of line. Its surface is highly reflective and its borrowed hues are vibrant… Snow assumes a great variety of colours, depending on the quality of light, and also on the sky, which it reflects. With the sun on your right or your left you see deep blue shadows on the surface of the snow wherever anything protects it from his rays. That is the blue of the zenith… Then, when the snow mantle lays in folds, some parts will borrow greener hues from the sky immediately above the horizon. And when the sun is low he radiates a warmer, rosier light, and shadow seems greener still within its contours… Those who have neglected to train their eyes to see the hues miss one of nature's most subtle manifestations of beauty! Snow changes colour constantly, in sympathy with its surroundings, particularly the sky, but so delicate is its colouration at all times that few of us are aware of it."[12]

TRAIL INFO

Trail information: The Bow Valley Parkway
Type of hike: Roadside view
Best time to go: Anytime
Distance: 50.7 km
Driving time: Allow 2 hrs so as to enjoy numerous stops along the drive
Topo map: 82 N/8, 82 O/5, 82 O/4
Route: The Bow Valley Parkway begins at a signed exit 5.6 km west of Banff. This road is a section of the original road from Banff to Lake Louise, which was built in 1920. The woodcut *Mountain Road* could be one of several places along the Parkway. Watch the scenery pass to try and place it exactly.

Belmore Browne
Rising Clouds, Lake Louise, undated
oil on canvas, Glenbow Collection

"BELMORE BROWNE DOES NOT PAINT A READY-MADE NATURE. HE BIDES HIS TIME AND AWAITS THE PSYCHOLOGICAL MOMENT, FOR THERE MAY BE MANY DAYS WHEN THE GREAT BROODING HEIGHTS LOOM SPHINX-LIKE, GUARDING THEIR SECRETS. THERE MAY BE WEEKS WHEN THE SNOW BARS THE PATH TO CONQUEST AND FORCES THE MAN OF ART TO SEEK REFUGE IN AN IMPOVERISHED SHELTER. MONTHS MAY PASS IN THE WILDERNESS WITHOUT THE SOUND OF A HUMAN VOICE — ONLY THE WEIRD CRY OF WILD BEASTS AND OF MOUNTAIN BIRDS, THE SOUND OF THE WIND, AND THE FRESH PINE SMELL OF APPROACHING SNOW."

— Anonymous exhibition leaflet, The Casson Galleries, undated

LAKE LOUISE AND AREA

RISING CLOUDS, LAKE LOUISE

Lake Louise, with the stunning Chateau, picturesque lake, magnificent mountains, and numerous glaciers, is probably the most visited spot in the Canadian Rockies. Since 1884, when the Canadian Pacific Railway built the wooden shack known as the Sumit [sic] Hotel, Lake Louise has attracted a steady and increasing stream of visitors. Among those visitors, since the earliest years, were artists.

In 1890, the CPR began to upgrade its facilities, and built a single-storey log chalet on the shore of Lake Louise. This chalet bears little resemblance to the massive structure now standing. Several fires have necessitated rebuilding, and subsequent additions have constantly changed the face of the world-famous Chateau Lake Louise. What has not changed is the magnificent view across the lake, which offers a stunning glacial panorama of the white face of Victoria Glacier and the angular ridges of Mount Lefroy and Lefroy Glacier.

The changing nature of the colours of the waters of Lake Louise has intrigued many artists, and the contrast of these fugitive blues against the starched white glacial backdrop is an irresistible scene. Belmore Browne, Frederic Marlett (F.M.) Bell-Smith, Walter Phillips, Carl Rungius, Peter Whyte, and Catharine Robb Whyte, all worked on the shores of Lake Louise and attempted to capture her fleeting dance of colour.

The trails that wind alongside the lake and up to Lake Agnes, Mirror Lake, the Big and Little Beehives, and Plain of the Six Glaciers were maintained by the CPR until 1952 when the Canadian National Parks system took them over. These trails have long allowed artists to work in close proximity to the glaciers and high passes that surround the Lake Louise region.

Frederic Marlett (F.M.) Bell-Smith
Morning, Lake Louise, 1909
watercolour on board, Glenbow Collection

"SOME OF MY PLEASANTEST RECOLLECTIONS ARE OF THE EARLY DAYS AT

LAKE LOUISE. MY FIRST VISIT TO THAT CHARMING SPOT WAS IN 1889, IN COMPANY

WITH MR. ALBERT BIERSTADT, OF NEW YORK, AN ARTIST VERY CELEBRATED

IN HIS DAY. THERE WAS THEN NO HOTEL THERE –

NOT EVEN A TRAIL TO THE LAKE, SO WE CARRIED BLANKETS, ETC.,

AND CAMPED ON THE LAKE SHORE AT THE VERY SPOT WHERE THE

MAIN ENTRANCE OF THE HOTEL OR CHATEAU NOW IS.

I REMEMBER ALSO THAT WE HAD THE PLEASURE OF MEETING THERE

COLONEL O'HARA, WHO CAMPED NEAR US AND WE SPENT

A PLEASANT EVENING ROUND THE CAMPFIRE. SINCE THEN,

I HAVE SEEN THE HOTEL GRADUALLY INCREASE IN SIZE FROM ONE

WHICH ONLY ACCOMMODATED TEN PERSONS.

AH! THOSE WERE THE DAYS. WE WERE LIKE A LITTLE FAMILY, AND

AGREEABLE FRIENDSHIPS WERE FORMED; BUT NOW EVERYTHING IS CHANGED."

— F.M. Bell-Smith, *Canadian Alpine Journal*, 1918

Belmore Browne
After September Snow (Lake Louise, Canadian Rockies), undated
oil on canvas, Glenbow Collection

> "THERE ARE HUNDREDS OF EMERALD LAKES, BUT THERE IS BUT ONE LAKE LOUISE."
>
> — Tom Wilson,
>   Banff outfitter, c.1884

MORNING, LAKE LOUISE

Frederic Marlett Bell-Smith worked as an illustrator and was a founding member of the Society of Canadian Artists (1867) and the Ontario Society of Artists (1872). He trained in England and continued his studies in Montreal and Hamilton after he immigrated to Canada with his family in 1866. He worked as a photographer in Toronto and Hamilton, and taught art in Ontario for ten years, after which he went to Paris to further his own painting studies. Paris energized and inspired him, and he put all his creativity into his painting, quickly gaining a solid reputation as an observant landscape painter. His work came to the attention of the Canadian Pacific Railway, and Bell-Smith went west in 1887 on a pass provided by the CPR, the fourth artist to do so that year.

Bell-Smith's watercolours are crisply executed and richly detailed, showing precision of line and limited, yet fully descriptive, brushwork. *Morning, Lake Louise,* is a clear watercolour depicting a small tent site pitched on the south shore and looking up towards Victoria Glacier. It conveys a wealth of information despite the economy of brushwork and detailing.

AFTER SEPTEMBER SNOW, LAKE LOUISE

This classic view of Lake Louise by Belmore Browne depicts a mountain snowfall in all its icy wet majesty. Mount Lefroy shows on the left with Mount Victoria peeking over Lefroy's shoulder. Browne was a master at painting the essence of coldness. A permeating, ice-forming, breath-freezing cold flows out of this canvas and envelopes you in sharp, still air. The deep blues of the frigid waters of Lake Louise are surrounded by the heavy whites of early autumn snow, whiter than the whites of winter because of the green contrasts that mark the turn of the season. In the sky, wind whips snow from the peaks of the mountains into puffs of ice above the glaciers.

Browne's work was composed on Louise's north shore, looking across the lake in a southwesterly direction, towards Mount Lefroy and Lefroy Glacier.

TRAIL INFO

Trail information:
Lake Louise
Type of hike: Half-day or day hike
Best time to go: Anytime; the height of summer will be the best time to view the colours shown in F.M. Bell-Smith's watercolour; fall, after an early snowfall, is best for Belmore Browne's oil. Lake Louise is wonderful in winter, and to fully appreciate the winter scene by Browne, take a cross-country ski trip along the Lakeshore trail or across the lake.
Trailhead: In front of the Chateau Lake Louise, leading west
Distance: 1.9 km to the west end of the lake
Elevation gain: None
Degree of difficulty: Easy
Hiking time: Allow 1 hour to walk the trail, more if you are adding other trails or activities
Topo map: 82 N/8
Route: If you follow the Lakeshore trail, you will be able to view the exact setting Browne painted this canvas from after a few minutes walk. The Bell-Smith scene is set from the southernmost end of the Lakeshore trail.

Thomas Fripp
Lake in the Clouds, Lake Agnes, Canadian Rockies, 1922
watercolour on paper, Collection of Don and Shirley Grace

LAKE IN THE CLOUDS, LAKE AGNES

Lake Agnes is set in a small cirque, a hollow high in a hanging valley above Lake Louise. The trail to the lake allows wonderful views of the surrounding valleys, and is an excellent hike for orienting yourself to the many trail systems in the Lake Louise area.

Lake Agnes was officially named in 1890 for Lady Agnes Macdonald, famous for her train ride on the cattle catcher of a Canadian Pacific locomotive, and for another Agnes, Agnes Knox, who was guided to the lake just a few days earlier than Mrs. Macdonald, usurping her attempt to become the first non-native woman to visit the lake. By lucky coincidence they were both named Agnes.

London-born Thomas Fripp first came to Lake Agnes in 1920, following his immigration to Canada in 1893. The son of a successful painter who taught him watercolour technique in a supportive, artistic environment, Fripp attended St. John's Wood Art School and the Royal Academy School in London. In Canada, he settled in British Columbia and took up farming, but suffered an accident and in 1904 decided to return full-time to the less perilous vocation of watercolour painting. He worked primarily on the British Columbia coast, and in the Alberta and British Columbia Rockies.

Fripp was a subtle colourist, exploring the slight tonal variations in particular colours such as grey and blue and the palest shades of green. His work would later impress printmaker Walter Phillips, who commented that:

"I delight chiefly in his grey effects — opalescent, delicate harmonies, envisaging the glories of grey. [Fripp] is unaffected by the many modern variants of watercolour technique and abides by the traditional methods of the English school. In this he is almost a group of one...."[13]

This delicate watercolour of Lake Agnes shows Fripp's keen sensitivity to the light and shadow conditions of the Rocky Mountains — the mountain face is indeed a delicate essay in grey. His aesthetic appreciation of the beauty of the region is apparent, and the work is filled with feeling and emotion. The wisps of snow-filled cloud are vigorous and alive and clamour across the lake, as the sun struggles to make itself felt through the weather. Fripp has captured Lake Agnes on a magical day, with her soft, clear, light blue waters that are characteristic of glacial-fed lakes. The sweeping strata of Mount Niblock forms a wonderful, upward-curving backdrop for the lake. Try to spend some time at Lake Agnes, as the clouds can often catch over the lake as Fripp has depicted them, and cause some marvelous light effects. The lake is a good spot for bird-watching, wildflowers, and wildlife.

TRAIL INFO

Trail information: Lake Agnes
Type of hike: Half-day hike
Best time to go: Late spring or early fall, when snow will be on the ground but the lake waters are open
Trailhead: Just off the Lakeshore trail, 200 m east of the Chateau (see Lake Louise Lakeshore trail information)
Distance: 3.4 km
Elevation gain: 380 m
Degree of difficulty: Easy to moderate
Hiking time: Allow 3 hrs
Topo map: 82 N/8
Route: Follow the Lakeshore trail to the west end of the Chateau and watch for the Lake Agnes trail sign at 200 m. You will begin with a steady uphill climb and reach the Mirror Lake junction at 2.6 km. Keep right for Lake Agnes. At 3 km the switchbacks begin, and at 3.1 km a second junction (the Little Beehive) is passed. You will climb a steep set of stairs, cross a bridge, and reach Lake Agnes at 3.4 km.

"IN REAL CREATIVE CONCENTRATION THE ARTIST IS OVER HIS HEAD, AS IT WERE,

AND IF THIS BECOMES SUFFICIENTLY INTENSE HE COMES UPON A

UNIQUE EXPERIENCE. HE MOVES INTO A PURE CREATIVE MOMENT WHICH IS

ABOVE LIFE AS WE KNOW IT. HE THEN BECOMES A CREATIVE AGENT,

A POWER AND NOT A PERSON. TO THE ARTIST, THIS MOST DESIRABLE MOMENT

IS NOT A RETREAT FROM REALITY, BUT REALITY ITSELF."

— Lawren Harris in *Canadian Comment on Current Events*, 1933

Lawren Harris in the Rockies,
1940-41

Lawren Harris
Mount Lefroy, 1930
oil on canvas, McMichael Canadian Art Collection

MOUNT LEFROY

In 1929, Group of Seven painter Lawren Harris took a sketching trip to the Rockies. He had been coming to the mountains to sketch for six years, and had painted landscapes from Mount Temple to Jasper. This trip would take him to Lake Louise and Mount Robson Provincial Park. In the time he had been coming to the mountains to paint, his work had undergone considerable stylistic change. The leap from a largely descriptive work such as *Emerald Lake* (p.92) to a comparatively abstract work such as *Mount Lefroy*, was a reflection of his deepening personal involvement in theosophy. Theosophy is a complex system of beliefs which rejects materialism and seeks purity within the framework of an ideal philosophical aesthetic. Theosophy also argues that knowledge and understanding of nature are more profound than empirical science can explain, and that spirituality is present in all things.

While painting in the Rockies, the mountains were Harris's symbolic foundation for ideas and thoughts, a "natural, albeit imperfect, metaphor…for the higher planes of spiritual existence through which each soul must pass."[14] He was not interested in depicting specific details of what he saw, and instead conveyed his vision of the highest elements of existence to others by presenting the essential spiritual aspects of what he saw. Arthur Lismer later said of him:

"He believes in the illusion of earth, the unreality of existence, and the presence of change. His blue-print for life is constantly undergoing change…but always with a purpose, to find a sort of perfection in living to prepare for a supreme perfection in a life beyond the senses and bodily existence. So his trees and houses and his lakes and clouds are part of an ordered unfolding plan — incomplete, imperfect — but creating endlessly new forms…It was inevitable that he should symbolize rather than represent. His abstractions…represent exquisite balance and movement, cosmic, slow, and spacious…He appeals to our sense of need for spiritual breathing space."[15]

Harris's field sketches were the starting point for many of his studio canvases. Elements that were a part of the actual landscape were often reshaped, restyled, or completely rejected during the process of working up the final works. These changes were often made in order to convey a higher, more spiritual, meaning. For instance, the field sketches for *Mount Lefroy* contain most of the geographical elements that actually exist in the region. Over the process of several intermediary studies and the final large canvas, The Mitre, the triangular feature to the left of Lefroy's peak, has gradually been stylized, reshaped, and even completely omitted. Harris's later work was to become completely abstract, although based on natural subjects, and was for him, the ultimate culmination of this personal quest.

In *Mount Lefroy*, Harris has selected the most triangular face of the mountain, and has worked its bands of ice and snow in clean, upward-thrusting shapes. Everything has been pared down to its geometric equivalent of the triangle, a conspicuous religious symbol, which at its most pluralistic and basic, represents the trinity and humankind's hope for paradise. Within theosophy, the triangle represents the elements of spirit, force, and matter. Harris often chose peaks that allowed him to explore this symbol, and found contemplating them a profound experience. Once, when hiking a strenuous trail with his friend and fellow Vancouver painter Bertram Charles (B.C.) Binning, Harris found himself extremely moved, and at the top of the peak:

"…in a trance-like state, he experienced glossalalia [speaking-in-tongues], and began an ecstatic, unintelligible chanting."[16]

"NO SCENE HAS EVER GIVEN ME AN EQUAL IMPRESSION
OF INSPIRING SOLITUDE AND RUGGED GRANDEUR.
I STOOD ON A GREAT STONE OF THE MORAINE WHERE,
FROM A SLIGHT ELEVATION, A MAGNIFICENT VIEW OF
THE LAKE LAY BEFORE ME, AND WHILE STUDYING THE
DETAILS OF THIS UNKNOWN AND UNVISITED SPOT,
SPENT THE HAPPIEST HALF-HOUR OF MY LIFE."

— Walter Wilcox, alpinist, 1899

MORAINE LAKE AND AREA

MORAINE LAKE

Moraine Lake was first seen by alpinists Walter Wilcox and Samuel Allen during their unsuccessful 1893 attempt to reach the summit of Mount Temple. They named the lake for the rockpile at its end, which present-day geologists believe is rockfall from Mount Babel, but which Wilcox insisted was a moraine. The name Moraine has stuck, and this tranquil lake has earned a reputation as a beautiful spot equal in charms to the better known Lake Louise, just a few kilometres to the north.

At the turn of the century, Banff outfitter Tom Wilson cut a rough trail above the lake, which in two years became an established CPR trail. The proximity of Moraine Lake to Lake Louise made it an obvious choice for a day-trip destination, and a carriage road was soon opened to allow visitors access to the quiet shores. By 1921, the road was open to cars. The CPR built a teahouse at Moraine Lake around 1912, and since then, as visitors to the lake have increased in number, the teahouse has become a lodge with additional cabins to catch the overflow of visitors from Lake Louise.

Kathleen (Kay) Daly was primarily a portrait and landscape painter. She was born in Ontario and attended the Ontario College of Art, studying under Arthur Lismer, J.E.H. MacDonald, and J.W. Beatty. She and husband artist George Pepper were close friends of A.Y. Jackson and Lawren Harris, and active in the formation of the Canadian Group of Painters who, subsequent to the Group of Seven, carried on the mandate of Canadian art based on Canada.

Daly travelled to various places in Canada to sketch, including the Rockies and the Arctic. She lived in Canmore from 1944 to 1946, where the natural sulphur springs of Banff eased her recovery from polio. While in Canmore, she painted the local life, the trappings of Canmore's mining industry, and the scenery of the surrounding mountains. At the time, her work was virtually unknown in western Canada, and it was not for several decades that her vision of the West was recognized. An exhibition of her work was mounted in 1987 at the Whyte Museum of the Canadian Rockies in Banff, and a reviewer remarked: *"These are not just paintings of mountains…These are our mountains…Somehow we know these paintings could only have been painted here. We smell pines and remember long trips through forests."*[17]

Daly's use of luminous colours characterize her mountain paintings. The blues and whites of the water depicted in *Moraine Lake* are rendered deep and compelling, a result of her careful observation of the nature of colour in glacial-fed lakes. The patterns of melt water entering the lake fade as they mix, settle out, and reach the near shore. These patterns blend ambiguously with the reflections of the peaks above. Daly's scene is set looking southwest down Moraine Lake from the Rockpile, a favourite vantage point for many painters. The central summits of the Ten Peaks can be seen, with their distinctive snow-filled chutes and scree slopes, marking the shoulder of each peak as it meets the next.

Kathleen Daly
Moraine Lake, undated
oil on canvas board, Glenbow Collection

FROM SEDIMENT TO PIGMENT
THE COLOURS OF GLACIAL-FED LAKES

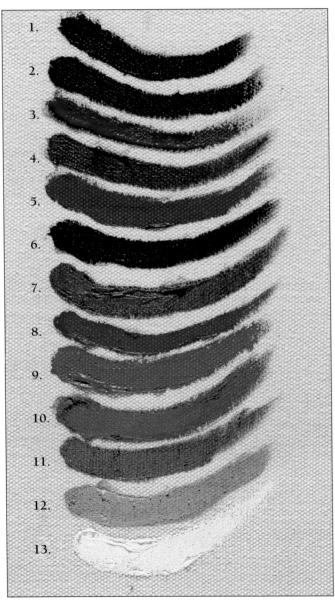

The waters of Moraine Lake, like so many lakes in the Rockies, consist mostly of glacial run-off; in Moraine's case, from the Wenkchemna Glacier. Ice, grinding against rock under incredible pressure as the glaciers move, produces a fine silt of rock flour, which runs with the melt waters down into the lakes. The density of the silt suspended in the lake determines the degree of light refraction through the water, and thus the colour.

At various times of the year, even at various times of the day, the amount of silt suspended in the water changes due to the increased or decreased flow from the glaciers. In mid-summer, when melting is at its peak, the lakes are heavily laden with silt, and the water is constantly stirred and churned by the force of the run-off. At this time of year, the waters look almost chalky, and take on a flat, pale viridian colour.

As the run-off lessens, the silt settles and the waters gradually clear, showing mid-tone cobalt blues and chrome greens mixed with the chalky patches where fresh run-off in the mountain streams enters the lake. The paths of these streams as they enter the lakes often stand out like a milky way running through the water.

At higher altitudes, small glacial lakes are as turquoise as the Caribbean, but to any who wish for the bathtub warm waters of south of the equator, be warned that the likeness ends with colour. These lakes are as cold as the North Sea. In the fall, after much of the silt has settled to the bottom, deep emerald greens, dark, clear violets, ultramarine blues, and cobalts predominate. When the waters are still, they can be as clear as glass. Underground springs, flowing through the Karst topography commonly found in the limestone throughout the Rockies, also feed these lakes, forcing additional clear waters into the mix. Excessive rain, mud and rock slides, wind, and wildlife stirring the water, and the composition, depth, and shape of the lake bottom all affect these colour variations, resulting in an ever-changing, infinitely diverse palette for the artist.

1. Violet
2. Viridian
3. Emerald Green
4. French Ultramarine
5. Ultramarine Blue
6. Prussian Blue
7. Chromium Oxide Green
8. Cobalt Blue
9. Cerulean Blue Medium
10. Cerulean Blue Light
11. Leaf Green
12. Ice Blue
13. Titanium White

Arthur J. Lismer
The Glacier, 1928
oil on canvas, Art Gallery of Hamilton

"THE WORLD OF APPEARANCES EXISTS, AS IT DOES TO THE RELIGIOUS DEVOTEE, AS A MEANS OF ECSTASY. A STEPPING OFF PLACE, AS IT WERE, INTO A WORLD WHEREIN THE DIVINE ORDER OF EXISTENCE, THE GOLDEN THREAD OF PURE DESIGN SHINES LIKE A PATHWAY OF FIRE IN THE REALM OF THE MIND, AND SPECULATION ON TECHNICAL AND OBJECTIVE THINGS IS REPLACED BY AESTHETIC CONTEMPLATION ON THE NATURE OF BEAUTY...ART ARISES FROM THE SPIRIT OF ADVENTURE LATENT IN MAN...A WORK OF ART IS LIKE THE LIFE OF MAN, FULL OF STRUGGLES, DIFFICULTIES AND SUFFERING, AND TO SHAPE IT [THE ARTIST] MUST LEAVE THE HIGHWAY AND BREAK NEW PATHS."

— Arthur Lismer in *Possession and Creation,*
  Ontario College of Art Student's Annual, c.1927

THE GLACIER

The valley system that surrounds the Moraine Lake area includes Sentinel Pass, Larch Valley, Paradise Valley, and Valley of the Ten Peaks. These regions offer an excellent variety of well-developed trails, endless hiking options, and exceptionally beautiful vistas of glaciers, alpine lakes, and peaks. Sentinel Pass is crested at 2611 metres by the highest maintained trail in the Canadian Rockies, and Paradise Valley is aptly named, with such delights as The Giant Steps, a system of waterfalls on Paradise Creek which descend over a series of large, rectangular rock bluffs, and the ten peaks of Wenkchemna visible from the trail as attractions. The Stoney Indian word for ten is Wenkchemna, a name sometimes applied to the Valley of the Ten Peaks, but officially only to Wenkchemna Pass.

Arthur Lismer's *The Glacier* depicts the rugged, glaciated peaks of Mount Fay in glowing, translucent colour. The halo of light that frames the pointed, uppermost peaks of the mountain and the sheer, bright ice that skirts the glacier which covers the mountain's face, convey a sense of cold austerity, remote and shimmering, like a precious jewel. Lismer's composition depicts the north face of Mount Fay and can be appreciated from several vantage points along the Sentinel Pass trail, in Larch Valley, and in the Valley of the Ten Peaks.

Although Arthur Lismer is known first and foremost as a founding member of the Group of Seven, he is also remembered as a powerful teacher. "I found I had the gift of the gab" he said, "and some scrapings of intellect that prompted me to teach."[18] His influence was felt not only in Canada, but through teaching fellowships in Italy, France, South Africa, and the United States. He taught two generations of artists, and his influence remains strong today.

Lismer's duties as a teacher deemed that painting expeditions be confined to the summer months:

"...just when the colour started to liven up he would have to pack up and go back to teaching, and so we miss in his canvases the seasonal changes which are depicted in the work of most Canadian artists... However, if he has been a summer painter, he has not painted pastorals. There are very few of his pictures wherein one could find pasture for a cow."[19]

In 1950, A.Y. Jackson wrote about Lismer in the magazine *Canadian Art*:

"Appreciation of Lismer's work has been slow in coming. To many people it seemed careless and untidy. His unconventional outlook was difficult to accept. He was never a follower; he has always blazed his own trails. We could think of a lot of artists who have had the same experience, and, because they were true to themselves, we honour their names above all others. May he continue for a long time to stir us out of lethargy and smugness, to put life into art education, to prod and exhort and inspire our younger generation and to take with good grace the slings and arrows and occasional bouquets that are the reward of a prophet." [20]

Lismer's devotion to the development of an art for our nation was steadfast. He said, when confronted with art in the English tradition that was being proffered as Canadian art, that:

"Canada is not like [England] and neither are its people. It is a country without shades and shadows, with bright colours and brutal changes of climate. Even the sun goes down with a bang …Changes occur abruptly … the blazing colours embody a sense of the power of Canadian Nature." [21]

In *The Glacier*, the sun has indeed gone down with a bang, leaving a strange otherworldly haze around Mount Fay.

In 1928, when Lismer first saw the Rockies, he was struck by the differences between the landscape of the mountains and the eastern landscape he had recently painted. He was also immediately aware of the different approach that he would need to master to be able to paint the mountains satisfactorily. He found himself suddenly forced out of "a sort of conventional pattern that crept into the work [of the Group of Seven]" [22] in their early years, a convention of undulating land and windswept pine and tangled colour.

Lismer found that in the mountains, the immediacy of the scene, the towering, imposing nature of the peaks, and the general predominance of structure over pattern, led him to a different kind of painting than the twisted and bent pines of Georgian Bay and Algonquin Park had inspired: "Mountains don't bend in the wind…they are cold and forbidding." [23] His remarkable adaptation to this new kind of scenery resulted in works like *The Glacier*, which is a thickly painted, solidly built-up

work, cold and impenetrable, with ice stacked on rock stacked on shadow, where the consistency of the sky is so tangible you feel that you could give it a little stir with your finger-tip.

Peter Whyte
From Larch Valley, Moraine Lake, undated
oil on canvas, Whyte Museum of the Canadian Rockies

FROM LARCH VALLEY, MORAINE LAKE

The fresh and lively works of Peter and Catharine Whyte are essential to an examination of the art of the Rocky Mountains. Peter Whyte was one of the first artists to paint his birthplace of Banff, where he took lessons from both Belmore Browne and Carl Rungius, painting with them in the field. In 1925, he painted at Lake O'Hara with the American landscape artist Aldro T. Hibbard, who encouraged Whyte to enroll in the School of the Museum of Fine Arts in Boston, where he met Catharine Robb. Before long they were secretly engaged. He returned to Banff, planning to meet her later in Europe where they would be married, after she completed her training at the Museum School. During this time, they wrote many letters back and forth, and his love of the mountains began to infect her. He writes:

"Crossing the plains it was intensely cold and the steam and water froze solid in our cars, making it rather uncomfortable for us. After we entered the mountains, things were not too bad, even though it did drop to 46° below zero. But, Kay, it seemed as though the Rockies were putting on a special day for me because I have never seen them with such wonderful colour, lights, shadows and such pure looking snow. They are real friends. I wish, Kay, that you could know them."[24]

After their marriage, the Whytes built a studio home in Banff which soon became the social centre of the community, and a regular stopping place for visitors to the town. Catharine noted one summer that they had entertained some 300 guests, and lamented the intrusion into their painting time. The balance between social and artistic life was difficult for them; Catharine often spoke of it in her letters to her mother. The very few large studio canvases by Peter, and none by Catharine, may have been the result of a lack of concentrated painting time.

The Whytes were involved in many activities in the community, particularly Banff's annual Indian Days celebrations. They were generous benefactors, community founders, and amiable hosts. The Whyte Museum of the Canadian Rockies, established by Catharine after Peter's death in 1966, now houses most of their work, as well as their extensive archive of personal correspondence, documents relating to the town of Banff, and a vast collection of mountain photographs.

Having lived so much of their lives in Banff, the Whytes looked at the mountains with an intimate eye, painting bold and clear renditions of familiar places. They sketched together all over the Rockies, and were each other's constant companions. In viewing their sketches, a sense of them as a couple is clearly felt, in fact one can determine that on a particular day, they sat about 20 feet apart, depicting the same panorama, noting the same patch of fireweed in bloom, the same twisted waterfall coursing with spring run-off.

The practicality of sketching in pairs in the Rockies cannot be overlooked, as two individuals can better attend to the hazards of changeable weather and silently approaching wildlife that might surprise an artist with eyes intent on work.

Catharine's prolific letters to her mother tell of many sketching trips, some successful, others not, that the couple took together throughout the Rockies. Yet despite the similarities in these "pairs" of sketches (in fact, later in her life, Catharine herself had trouble telling her own work from Peter's), distinct differences often appear. Catharine's work is often more painterly — free in brushwork and loose in handling — than Peter's, which tends to be more orderly, flatter, carefully composed, and laid out. She chose close-up scenes more often, concentrating on the detail of rocks, clouds rolling over peaks, pools of water, while his sketches more often show a larger scene, with a set fore, middle, and background.

Catharine Robb Whyte
On the Rock Pile, Looking West (Wenkchemna), undated
oil on canvas, Whyte Museum of the Canadian Rockies

"IT'S VERY HARD TO FINISH A CAREFUL SKETCH IN ONE

SITTING…FOR THE LIGHT CHANGES SO RAPIDLY IN

THE MOUNTAINS."

— Catharine Robb Whyte to her mother, Edith Robb, 1941

ON THE ROCK PILE, LOOKING WEST, WENKCHEMNA

Catharine's sketch is composed, as the title denotes, from the rockpile at Moraine Lake looking west into the Valley of the Ten Peaks. The Whytes produced many sketches of the Louise region, as the trip from Banff to Lake Louise was short and could be made easily when the Whytes had only a few days to sketch. It was also a convenient stop on the way to or from Lake O'Hara or Bow Lake, two of the Whytes' other favourite painting spots.

Despite the quickness of Catharine's sketches, she often complained in her letters to her mother that she had trouble completing a sketch in one sitting. She was very observant of colour, and interested in the subtle variations light caused in the colours of wet rock, snow, and in water. Catharine's sketches often contain predominate sky-scapes, contrasting strongly with scenes that Peter painted, even on the same day, in which the sky does not appear as turbulent and alive. Catharine's nephew Jon Whyte, a writer and historian, later noted:

"When I read the diaries Catharine wrote when she was a teenager, I understood, as I had not before, that her sketches' often stormy skies embody her strong emotions. People may read her landscapes as simple depiction, but this always dynamic, congenial, considerate, charitable, and democratic woman, her face illuminated by a smile and her love of life, created pictures surprising to us who thought we knew her. The tension created by a serene foreground lake and a storm-threatened sky excites her; such themes are revealing self-portraits."[25]

Although Peter was supported and encouraged strongly by Catharine, and by artists J.E.H. MacDonald, Aldro Hibbard, Lawren Harris, Walter Phillips, and Banff's Belmore Browne and Carl Rungius, his career never really blossomed. He had few exhibitions of his work and he did not teach. He was also an alcoholic. Lawren Harris became a friend of the Whytes and was aware of Peter's talent. The Whytes and Harris began to correspond and, eventually, Catharine voiced her concern over Peter's stalled career. Harris wrote back to Catharine, expressing openly his opinion on the major hindrance to Peter's artistic career:

"I have thought a good deal about your situation and think I see where the difficulty is… In order to make this clear… I will have to be very frank. In the first place Peter must get off to a new start in painting. This he cannot possibly do in Banff. He has the equipment, the technique, the talent to do far better work than he has ever done. He has simply

*been bogged down in Banff...
Artists might retire there after a
lifetime of endeavor somewhere
else, but creatively they wither
however easy and pleasant the
life... I feel that you have to get
out of Banff as soon as possible
and stay away for two or three
years — make a complete break
— even sell your house. Peter
will never get anywhere in Banff.
...He has however a very good
chance of getting away to a new
start, a new outlook on life and
the best productive period he has
ever had if you get out of
Banff... When you get away to
New York or wherever it is,
Peter should be put under the
care of a doctor...join
alcoholics anonymous...see him
through to a real cure. One of
these without the other isn't
enough. There must be a new
creative venture in art, a new life
— and there must also be a cure
from alcoholism."[26]*

Harris's honest, candid
opinion probably shocked
Catharine and he writes again to
her one month later, softening
the tone of his comments, and
politely conceding to her
understanding of the problems
of family life. The Whytes
never did leave Banff, and
Peter's alcoholism went
untreated. In her gentile,
democratic way, Catharine
rarely mentions the illness
despite the intimacy of her
letters.

TRAIL INFO

Trail information: Valley of
the Ten Peaks (Moraine
Lake to Wenkchemna Pass)
Type of hike: Day hike
Best time to go: Anytime
Trailhead: The Moraine
Lake parking lot
Distance: 9.7 km
Elevation gain: 712 m
Degree of difficulty:
Moderate
Hiking time: Allow 6 hrs
Topo map: 82 N/8
Route: Follow the Moraine
Lake Shoreline trail to the
Sentinel Pass/Wenkchemna
junction at 350 m. Steep
switchbacks make up the
next 2 km, but endure as
the trail is moderate after
you reach the next junction
(there's a bench!) which
leads to Larch Valley and
Sentinel Pass at 2.5 km.
Moraine Lake is visible
through the trees, shining
in all her glorious colours.
At 6 km you pass Eiffel
Lakes, watch for views that
approximate Peter Whyte's
composition from here. You
will reach Wenkchemna
Pass at 9.7 km.
Optional trails: A shorter
hike to the top of the
Rockpile will also give
you a classic view of
Moraine Lake. Take the
trail that follows Moraine
Creek to Consolation
Lakes. You will climb a
short hill, keep right at
the Consolation Lakes
junction.

"DON'T YOU KNOW THAT JUST SIX INCHES BEYOND YOUR
TOES THERE ARE 4,500 FEET OF PERPENDICULAR AIR —
AND THAT I DON'T WANT TO STEP ON IT?"

— Walter Wilcox to guide, *Canadian Alpine Journal*, 1894

MOUNT FAIRVIEW FROM
MOUNT TEMPLE

Thomas Fripp's ethereal,
almost supernatural watercolour, *Mount Fairview from
Mount Temple*, will entice
experienced climbers and
lovers of the remote to the
uppermost regions of Mount
Temple, a popular climb since
the first ascents of Walter
Wilcox and Samuel Allen in
1894.

Mount Temple is the highest
peak in the Lake Louise area,
with a summit towering 1700
vertical metres above the
village of Lake Louise to the
northeast, Larch Valley and
Moraine Lake to the south, the
Valley of the Ten Peaks to the
southeast, and the Horseshoe
Glacier to the west. It sports a
full range of climbing routes,
including an easy climb which
Gregory Horne's *Selected
Climbing Routes of Mount
Temple* calls "a scramble."
Untrained climbers should be
cautioned about this scramble
as Mount Temple has claimed

more than its share of lives.
Rock falls and ice avalanches
are a common occurrence on
this massive peak and can
happen at any time of year.

Perhaps Fripp's depiction of
the wind-whipped summits
of Mount Temple and Fairview
Mountain is cautionary
enough. The cold, dry light
that strains through the
snow-filled air, illuminating
the rocks in careful detail on
Mount Temple, and secreting
them in a white veil of cold on
Fairview Mountain, does not
invite a trail-side picnic.
Fairview Mountain, which
looms close in the watercolour,
is actually some 4.8 kilometres
away from Mount Temple
across Paradise Valley.

Thomas Fripp
Mount Fairview from Mount Temple, 1918
watercolour on paper, Glenbow Collection

Lawren Harris
Mount Temple, undated
oil on heavyweight laminate board
McMichael Canadian Art Collection

"THE CONTEMPLATION OF VISIBLE NATURE AND THE RENDERING OF NATURAL SCENES AND EFFECTS COME TO DEMAND THE USE OF HIGH POWERS OF SELECTION AND ARRANGEMENT, AND EVENTUALLY BY WAY OF SIMPLIFICATION OF THE NATURALISTIC TO ITS FUNDAMENTAL AND PUREST FORM WE ACHIEVE THE UNITY OF CREATIVE VISION. SO IT IS THAT OUR VISION IS SLOWLY CLARIFIED AND WE COME TO SEE NATURE IN A NEW AND UNIFYING LIGHT."

— Lawren Harris papers, National Archives of Canada, 1920

THE TRANS-CANADA HIGHWAY

MOUNT TEMPLE

Magnificent Mount Temple towers its 3544 metre summit over the Lake Louise area and can be seen from many hiking trails in the adjacent valleys, from the banks of the Bow River, along the Trans-Canada Highway, up the Icefields Parkway, and south towards Banff. This impressive peak was named for Sir Richard Temple (1862 – 1902), a British economist who actually did very little travelling in the Rockies. The literal denotation of the word temple does better justice to the peak than does the namesake of Sir Richard, as it is a climber's shrine and a mountain devotee's altar. It was an ideal mountain for a painter as spiritually oriented as Lawren Harris, who saw it as a universal symbol of humankind's humility. It is massive, snow-capped, soaring, and remote, dwarfing everything in its domain.

Harris saw such peaks as a touching off point between the earthly world and the divine. He has painted Mount Temple thrusting unfettered through weightless clouds, sheer bands of light that shroud the peak, almost as if it were ascending to the heavens.

TRAIL INFO

Site information: Mount Temple
Type of hike: Roadside view
Best time to go: Any time of year, in clear weather
Topo map: 82 N/8
Route: Mount Temple is situated about halfway between Moraine Lake and Lake Louise. It is the dominant peak in the Bow Range because of its massive size, and impressive glaciers, but the whole range in which Temple is found is stunning. Mount Temple can be seen from several places along the road. Heading out from Lake Louise, the road northeast to Jasper provides stunning views of Temple in the first 3 km. If you are returning to Lake Louise from Jasper, watch for Temple from the hilly section before Herbert Lake. The Icefields Parkway Interpretive Exhibit is a good place to stop. Heading towards Banff from Lake Louise, the views are best immediately upon reaching the Trans-Canada Highway. The section of the Bow Valley Parkway nearest to Lake Louise and the Lake Louise Ski Area roads all provide good perspectives.

Barbara Mary (Barleigh) Leighton
Mount Eisenhower, undated
colour woodcut on paper, Glenbow Collection

CASTLE MOUNTAIN

Among the many couples who painted together in the Rockies were Barbara and Alfred Crocker (A.C.) Leighton. Barbara was a student at Tech (later the Alberta College of Art and Design or ACAD) when she met and married A.C. in the 1930s. Their unconventional life together was one of adventures in painting and of founding roles in the development of the arts in Alberta:

"A.C. didn't think much of wedding ceremonies so the marriage wasn't announced until the day before — so no one would come. The ceremony was held at seven a.m. — so no one would come. The marriage certificate went into the nearest wastebasket… As for the reception…everyone came — except the bride and groom. By the time it started, they had collected their waiting horses and had ridden into the hills for a six-week painting expedition."[27]

Barbara was extremely supportive of A.C.'s career and felt that: *"There can be only one landscape artist in a family…you have to be ready to drop everything and go where the landscape is. Like the afternoon A.C. finished a particularly arduous assignment in Calgary and booked a flight to Ireland the following morning."*[28] They left the breakfast dishes in the sink for three years.

To supplement their income during the Depression, A.C. taught Barbara the technique of woodblock printing, and she began to make colour prints based on his paintings, signing them with the name "Barleigh." They had plans of editioning 100 of each print, but they did not sell as well as the Leightons had hoped, and did not help their financial situation to any degree.

After A.C.'s death in 1965, Barbara turned her attention to her own career and returned to school. She continued to produce woodblock prints based on A.C.'s watercolours, each being composed of images cut from between ten and fifteen blocks, one for each colour or group of colours. Each stage of the work is done by hand: drawing, tracing, cutting, and printing, a painstaking, lengthy process. The blocks are cut in relief, leaving only the raised parts that will be inked to print the various shapes that fit together, like a puzzle, to create an image.

Barbara also printed using the linoleum block technique, as well as working in fabric and metal. She received her diploma in Fine Art Crafts from the Alberta College of Art in 1969.

Barbara had worked as a landscape gardener in Calgary prior to 1930, and her "gardener's eye" shows in her woodblock prints. The trees and shrubs in the middle ground of *Mount Eisenhower* have been "landscape designed," the soft fall colours organized carefully against the hazy blues of the mountain in complementary harmony, perfectly balanced.

Barbara was elected a Full Member of the Canadian Society of Painters-Etchers and Engravers in 1941, and her prints are found in numerous collections across Canada and in the United States.

TRAIL INFO

Trail information:
Castle Mountain
(Mount Eisenhower)
Type of hike:
Roadside view
Best time to go: Fall, in clear weather
Topo map: 82 O/5
Route: Castle Mountain was originally named for its turreted and fortress-like appearance, but was renamed Mount Eisenhower in honour of General and United States President Dwight D. Eisenhower in 1946, much to the displeasure of Canadians. The name was changed back to Castle Mountain in 1979, but the eastern-most turret has retained the name Eisenhower Peak. The perspective that Barbara Leighton has used for this work is best viewed from the Bow Valley Parkway or the Trans-Canada Highway, between Johnston Canyon and Castle Junction. There are a number of pull-outs along the way, and the mountain is so massive the view approximates the art for several kilometres.

Lars Jonson Haukaness
Ptarmigan Pass, Canadian Rockies, 1928
oil on canvas, Collection of Don and Shirley Grace

SKOKI

PTARMIGAN PASS, CANADIAN ROCKIES

The Skoki region east of Lake Louise is an area of unlimited exploration, with 16 lakes, five passes, unending alpine meadows, and abundant wildlife. A geologist's dream and a botanist's fantasy, fossils and formations are side by side with flowers of every type, a fact that is witnessed by the area's place names: Brachiopod Mountain, Myosotis (the genus name for Forget-Me-Not) Lake, Fossil Mountain. Skoki's environs are as varied as the artists who worked there: Carl Rungius, avid sportsman and impressionistic wildlife painter; watercolourist A.C. Leighton; printmaker Walter Phillips; and Norwegian landscape painter and portraitist Lars Haukaness. The region has been a backcountry ski destination since 1930, and is the site of the first lodge built specifically for skiing in the Canadian Rockies.

In 1919, Lars Haukaness came to Winnipeg from Chicago, where he had been living intermittently since his immigration to the United States from Norway in 1888, making a living as a travelling portraitist. He had attended private art school in Oslo (then Christiania), as well as the Norwegian Royal Academy School, and was exposed to the fundamentals of European impressionism. He participated in a number of exhibitions, both in Norway and in the United States, and entered a work in the Paris Salon of 1905. His work blends elements of impressionism and naturalism in landscapes that convey both the physical topography and the mood and feeling of the place they depict.

In 1926, he went to Calgary, and immediately began to paint in the Rockies, depicting Moraine Lake, Lake Louise, and the Ptarmigan Lake area near Skoki. That year he taught a class at the Calgary Art Club, and in 1927 was invited to teach an art class at Tech, which was concentrating on retraining veterans at the time, and giving little attention to formal art instruction. Immediately, Haukaness began to sever connections with the technical side of the school, and work to establish a provincial school of art.[29] He had grand schemes for a fully autonomous school, schemes that initiated action, but would not be realized in his lifetime. Haukaness is, however, credited with founding what is now the Alberta College of Art and Design.

During the summers, he went to the Rockies to paint, preferring more and more the Ptarmigan Valley on the trail to Skoki, where he went repeatedly for backcountry painting expeditions. The topography of the region might have appealed to his Norwegian sensibilities, as the flat stillness of Ptarmigan Lake, gently reclining in the rolling, treeless, alpine meadows that surround it, is in many ways similar to the mountain landscape of Norway.

Haukaness planned his painting trips in between teaching responsibilities, and in July of 1929, set out for Ptarmigan Lake from Lake Louise. A few days before he left for the sketching trip, he had met Archie Key, who later wrote an article about Haukaness, which profiles the artist and provides a few details as to his mountain sketching gear:

"He was an elderly man with a yellowish-white beard and dressed in an old grey coat, khaki riding breeches and puttees. Behind his spectacles which perched insecurely on his nose, there was a humorous twinkle in his eyes. He was full of enthusiasm, preparing to leave for a sketching trip in the Canadian Rockies, but he was disconcerted because he had lost his pinto. His pack horse and his dog were a few blocks away, and as he talked about the loss of his saddle pony... he reminded me of Don Quixote making preparations for a journey of adventure... He pulled out tacks and rolled up the rough material with other partly finished sketches. His paints and brushes, palette and knives were included in the bundle and the whole were wrapped up in old newspapers and securely tied with rope."[30]

While at the lake, Haukaness died suddenly, apparently of a heart attack. The notice of his death in the *Calgary Herald* on September 6, 1929, read:

"While riding to Lake Louise, after having been stricken mortally ill with heart disease in his lonely teepee in Ptarmigan Valley, Lars Haukaness, 66 years of age, noted painter and instructor for two years at the Institute of Technology and Art, fell dead from his horse about three miles from the resort, early Wednesday morning. His dog, 'Bragg,' returning to the town without his master, gave the police a clue to the tragedy."[31] Haukaness is buried in Banff.

Alfred Crocker (A.C.) Leighton
Boulder Pass, Skoki, 1935
watercolour on paper, Private Collection

BOULDER PASS

A.C. Leighton had been active in the British Royal Academy since age 17, painting watercolours according to the formalities of conservative composition and use of colour, light, and subject matter. His English subjects had included pastoral farm and river scenes, street scenes and architectural subjects, and scenes of windmills and sluice gates, typical in their rustic British sensibilities. Leighton's conservative style, when used to depict the Rockies, was just what the CPR officials were looking for to entice European immigrants and easterners to the West. The wild drama of the looming Canadian mountains might appear more welcoming if washed with a familiar British brush. But for Leighton, the British tendencies of his brush soon found the Canadian scenery a challenge. The panorama was limitless, with expansive views in every direction, and he found he had to adapt his painting format to accommodate the splendor of the mountains:

"The grandeur of the scenery, the purity and the beauty of the colouring being indescribable, there was no lack of subject, for one could be found at every angle. The scale of the landscape was tremendous. I soon found that a 14 x 10 inch [surface] was too small even to rough in composition, and something much larger was necessary to portray the magnitude, the imposing force and dignity of those mountains."[32]

His love for the Rockies grew, and to his delight the CPR sent him west a second time. This time, he left the boundary of the rail line and hiked further up into the Rockies, exploring alpine regions and peaks. He began to expand his repertoire to include dramatic settings and to express the wilder qualities of such scenery, particularly in his watercolours.

Leighton was an adventurous artist, happy to "rough it" in pursuit of the perfect vista, the perfect season, the perfect light. Sleeping on top of his food to keep it from freezing, persisting with frozen paints and rearing horses, and trying, almost always, to paint on the spot, Leighton attacked the mountains. Once, although the train conductor was willing to stop to let him off wherever he chose, he took the quick way off the train when he saw a choice painting spot flash by. Weighted down with a pack full of brushes and paints, he leapt from the train just as it emerged from the Spiral Tunnels in the Yoho Valley. He lost his balance and fell over the cliff he had tried to land on, tumbling down the side. Cut and bruised but with paintbox and canvas still intact, he managed to limp his way into the nearby village of Field, much to the surprise of the party setting out with a stretcher to rescue him.

Leighton's paintings of the Rocky Mountains, particularly the remote, alpine regions and high, desolate passes, are considered to be among the best of his work. Leighton's access to the Rockies began with his CPR pass in 1924, but he reached the high altitude sites through membership in the Trail Riders of the Canadian Rockies Club, which he joined during his second painting trip with the railway in 1927. With the Trail Riders, he visited Lake O'Hara, the Yoho Valley, and Mount Assiniboine, exploring the rocky trails of glacial moraines, alpine meadows, and windswept summits.

When he married artist Barbara Harvey, they began to seek even more remote painting locations, desiring complete solitude. A.C. Leighton was rather "high-strung," and disliked any aspect of civilization intruding on the peace of his painting expeditions; the sound of trains in valleys below or motorcars on access roads, even the noises of pack horses, were intolerable. The couple eventually abandoned the Trail Riders in favour of trekking into remote camps for extended stays. They would secure the help of an outfitter who would drop them off with ample supplies and pick them up two or three weeks later. Alone, they could enjoy quietude and solitude and concentrate uninterrupted on painting.

Alfred Crocker (A.C.) Leighton
Mount Skoki, 1935
oil on canvas, The Leighton Foundation

"I PAINT BECAUSE I MUST. I PAINT FROM 12 TO 14 HOURS DAILY. WHEREVER I GO I SEE SOMETHING TO PAINT — FLOWERS, BEER BOTTLES — ANYTHING. IT IS A DISEASE."

— A.C. Leighton in *The Albertan*, 1956

MOUNT SKOKI

By 1935, Leighton, who had worked primarily in watercolour, had begun to work in oil, and that year he and Barbara packed into Skoki for a painting trip. During this time, he painted studies for the canvas *Mount Skoki*, which was exhibited by the Royal Canadian Academy (RCA) in 1935.[33] The oil now hangs permanently over the fireplace at the home the Leightons built in the Alberta foothills, now a historic site, gallery, and program centre.[34]

For Leighton, *Mount Skoki* was an early exploration in oil, and a work that charts the gradual transition from his conservative water-colours, to a more expressive, naturalistic approach to the mountains. *Mount Skoki* still has much in common with his work in watercolour, the characteristic sobriety, quiet tones, and careful composition are the backbone of the work. The usual devices of foreground, centre stage, and backdrop support this cast of features.

The work is a remarkably sensitive oil when one considers the nature of the topography of the Skoki region, and in particular, Skoki Mountain itself. The 2707 metre summit is free of permanent snowfield or glacier, perhaps a feature which makes it less picturesque than other peaks whose surfaces are dramatized by the effects of glacial ice. Melt waters, reflected light, and powerful white/dark con-trasts are absent. The Paleozoic carbonate rock of which the mountain is composed is quite sombre and even in colour. The mountain is set apart from the surrounding peaks, resulting in less shadow play and a feeling of openness, quite opposite to a location such as Lake O'Hara or Mount Robson. Yet the subtleties of the mountain's pinkish tones and the rhythmic undulations of the peaks are sympathetically rendered by Leighton, and show a critical eye and careful palette.

Carl Rungius
Brachiopod Mountain, undated
oil on canvas, Glenbow Collection

Carl Rungius
Ptarmigan Peak, undated
oil on canvas, Glenbow Collection

"FOR REALLY FINE [MOUNTAIN] SCENES,

GET TEXTURE OF ROCKS USING SAND IN PAINT. ALSO

USE A VERY SCRUFFY BRUSH TO TEXTURE THE PAINT.

PAINT FIRST COAT (TEXTURE COAT) WITH A FAST

DRYING PAINT OF OIL AND SAND MIXED IN

FOREGROUND TREES, ROCKS, AND [MOUNTAINS].

NO SAND IN SKY OR WATER."

— Carl Rungius papers, Glenbow Museum Archives, 1959

BRACHIOPOD MOUNTAIN PTARMIGAN PEAK

The artwork depicting big game by painter Carl Rungius is well-known to followers of the genre, but lesser known in the broader realm of Canadian art. Walter Phillips, who wrote about Rungius in the *Winnipeg Tribune*, wondered at the fact that although Rungius's art "is essentially Canadian in subject and spirit, it is almost unknown in the country."[35] Even lesser known than his big game subjects are Rungius's landscape field studies, the majority of which were done in the Canadian Rockies between Banff and Jasper.

Rungius studied at the Berlin Academy of Arts from 1888 to 1890. He honed his animal anatomy drawing skills at this time by spending hours drawing at the zoo and from horse carcasses in a local glue factory. In 1894, he was invited to visit an uncle in the United States who took him moose hunting in Maine. He returned to the United States permanently the following year, this time to the Wyoming mountains, enticed by the advertising of a sportsman's show leaflet. Rungius was dazzled by the wildlife, scenery, and great expanses he encountered,

and began his lifetime of painting in North America.

He started to travel on his own in the American Rockies, hunting and sketching in Wyoming, and set up a studio in Greenpoint, New York, to work his field studies into larger canvases. He went to the Yukon in 1904 to hunt and sketch, and later to New Brunswick in search of moose. Rungius had come to North America during the Golden Age of Illustration, a time when inexpensive, illustrated magazines proliferated. Wildlife and sporting magazines were extremely popular, and Rungius found a ready market in New York for his work. He soon became an artist celebrity, and his work illustrated the covers of *Field and Stream*, *American Sportsman*, and several other popular sporting magazines.

In 1910, Banff outfitter and guide Jimmy Simpson became aware of Rungius's work through *The New York Zoological Society Bulletin*, which reproduced one of Rungius's paintings on its cover. Simpson was an amateur artist himself, and interested in art depicting the animals and landscape of his native Rockies. He had guided a number of artists in the Rockies, sometimes waiving his fee in favour of a painting. He wrote to Rungius, inviting him for a complimentary hunt.

In August of that year, Rungius arrived in Banff, and Simpson took him north along the Bow River to Bow Lake, into the Mistaya Valley, along the North Saskatchewan River, and up to the Columbia Icefields. They hunted, Rungius sketched, and the prolific big game and expansive scenery of the area took hold of him. The trip affected his painting dramatically, and from this point on in his career, landscape began to be as important an element within his art as his animal subjects:

"For the first time I felt the urge to paint straight landscape; until then I had felt the landscape only as a setting for big game. But the grandeur of the mountains, with marvelous atmospheric conditions, changed all that. Wyoming was too dry and photographic; New Brunswick just woodlands; and my stay in the Yukon was too short. I felt I had found my country."[36]

Simpson and Rungius became good friends, and Rungius became a regular client. In 1921, Rungius built a summer studio home in Banff on the road to the Cave and Basin Hot Springs. Rungius and his wife Louise named the studio "The Paintbox" and Rungius painted there from April to mid-October each year.

In 1923, Rungius joined the newly-formed Trail Riders of the Canadian Rockies club, which organized a yearly trail ride and awarded mileage pins to its members. In 1928, he became the club's president.

In addition to pure landscape, Rungius continued to hunt and paint big game, and expanded his territory north to the Jasper region with outfitter Jim Boyce in the 1930s. It was there that he painted some of his most famous works along the Clearwater and Ram rivers.

TRAIL INFO

Trail information: Skoki
Type of hike: Long day trip, cross country ski, or overnight backpack
Best time to go: All of the artworks listed in this section were executed in the summer and fall
Trailhead: Fish Creek parking lot, on the Temple Ski Lodge access road, 1 km from its junction with the Whitehorn Road to the main ski area
Distance: 15.6 km to the Merlin Meadows campground from Lake Louise Ski Area
Elevation gain: 790 m
Degree of difficulty: Easy to moderate
Hiking time: Allow 4 hrs
Topo map: 82 N/8, 82 N/9
Route: The trail begins just past Temple Ski Lodge. If you are a guest of Skoki Lodge, you will be driven up the 3.9 km access road from Fish Creek parking lot by bus. Otherwise, you must hike or bike this portion of the trail. In the winter, you can take the ski lifts to Eagle Ridge and ski over to Temple Lodge. The trail to Boulder Pass begins 200 m up the ski run east of the lodge. At 7.1 km you will reach the Halfway Hut. Stop here and look up the pass towards Fossil Mountain. This is the best location from which to observe the view depicted in Leighton's watercolour *Boulder Pass — Skoki*. The semi-permanent snow on Fossil Mountain is a good reference point with which to get your bearings within the painting. Continue up the Boulder Pass trail; at 8.6 km you will crest Boulder Pass at the west end of Ptarmigan Lake. The junction at 10.5 km leads left up Deception Pass and into Skoki, or right to Brachiopod Mountain on the Baker Lake trail. No obvious trail up Brachiopod Mountain exists, but occasional cairns and the intermittent trails of previous explorers can be followed to view the site of Rungius's oil sketch of Brachiopod Mountain. A lucky few might find the rock used by an artist (perhaps Rungius) as a palette, still in place on the slopes of Brachiopod Mountain.[37] Remarkably, the pigments have withstood more than 50 years of the area's notorious weather. Returning to the main trail to Skoki, at 11 km you will crest Deception Pass. Continue over the pass, and your view of Skoki Mountain will roughly echo Leighton's depiction of it. The soft pinks and warm browns of the mountain are especially muted in the evening and in fall, when the light is low and shadows are long. The fluted peaks on Skoki's southern slope are exactly rendered, and depicted from a direct, head-on perspective. At the 13.9 km junction, keep straight for Skoki Lodge at 14.4 km and the Merlin Meadows campground at 15.6 km.

"IT HAS COMMENCED TO SNOW AGAIN…

SO IT IS IMPOSSIBLE TO PAINT AT PRESENT.

THE SCENERY IS WONDERFUL, INDEED NO ONE

COULD IMAGINE ANYTHING LIKE IT. IT IS A TERRIBLE

JOB TO KEEP WARM AND IF ONE DOES NOT KEEP

ON THE MOVE IT IS IMPOSSIBLE."

— A.C. Leighton journal entry, 1927

Alfred Crocker (A.C.) Leighton
Mount Assiniboine, undated
oil on linen, The Edmonton Art Gallery

Barbara Mary (Barleigh) Leighton
Mount Assiniboine, undated
colour woodcut on paper, Glenbow Collection

"IT RISES, LIKE A MONSTER TOOTH, FROM AN

ENTOURAGE OF DARK CLIFF AND GLEAMING

GLACIER..."

— James Outram, alpinist and writer in
  The Alpine Journal, 1902

MOUNT ASSINIBOINE

In 1991, Mount Assiniboine Provincial Park was designated a World Heritage Site. It is truly an area of worldwide acclaim, with the massive face of Mount Assiniboine watching over the surrounding lakes, peaks, and passes. Rolling alpine meadows carpeted with the nodding white heads of avens in spring, which turn and twist upright into rusty pink flames as the fall days approach, cover the surrounding valleys. Little lakes are tucked here and there, and always seem to present themselves just as you are ready for lunch.

Steep passes and valleys that smell of berries and bears lead in and out of the Mount Assiniboine region. In winter, it is a cross-country ski paradise, with the rolling slopes waist deep in powder, clear crisp days, and broad expanses of untracked blue and white. Visitors should allow enough time in the region of the "Matterhorn of the Rockies" to fully explore during the day, and to return to the foot of this striking peak for a night or two at least. It is a picture perfect mountain, poking its sharp, triangular horn, often clad with persistent clouds, into the backstage of most views for miles in every direction.

The mountain was named by George Mercer Dawson, of the Geological Survey of Canada, in 1884, and since that time its reputation has spread worldwide to climbers, hikers, artists, and explorers. A lodge was built by the CPR in 1928 on the meadow above Lake Magog looking across to Mount Assiniboine, and was run by Erling Strom in the winter from 1928 to 1975. He recalled guiding a woman into the lodge and carrying her heavy wooden paintbox, loaded with supplies, all the way from Banff. Upon arrival at Assiniboine, he found out that she had never painted before. "Fine place to start," he said, "I'm glad you didn't want to try to learn the piano."[38] Artists can now fly their paintboxes in by helicopter.

During his time as an artist for the CPR, A.C. Leighton discovered Assiniboine. He would return to the region several times in his painting career, as he found the scenery exactly to his liking. His first trip, in 1927, was plagued by heavy snow, and attempts to paint were thwarted when his watercolours froze, so he switched to pastels:

"Have just returned from making a sketch," reads his journal entry. *"I walked out to find a subject and thought I could sit for a short while so did a quick pastel, taking about 20 minutes. After that I began to get cold. It was snowing most of the time but one can blow it off quite easily like dust and it does not bother much."*[39]

It seems that keeping warm on the trip was his biggest challenge, and presented him with far more difficulty than did sketching. Using whatever he had on hand to keep warm, he found that his sketching paper made excellent insulation, and stuffed it in between two layers of socks. On a corner of a page in his journal he records a shopping list for later, which includes quantities of two types of paper.

Despite the fact that some of his art supplies found other uses, Leighton was very satisfied with the results of the Assiniboine trip, and completed nearly one dozen sketches during his eleven-day stay, depicting what he thought to be "some of the most fascinating scenery in the world."[40] The snow was unrelenting, and he wrote upon arrival back in Banff on October 12:

"When I arrived my outside clothing which was covered with snow had turned to ice, like a suit of armour and tin hat. We made camp tonight in the dark. The food we had brought was all frozen."[41]

Peter Whyte
Mount Assiniboine, September Snow, c.1941
oil on canvas, Whyte Museum of the Canadian Rockies

"WE WAITED ALL LAST WINTER FOR ONE STORM HALF THE SIZE OF THIS AND NEVER GOT IT SO [PETER] WAS DELIGHTED. IT REALLY IS LOVELY THE TREES SO BOWED DOWN WITH SNOW AS THERE HAS BEEN NO WIND."

— Catharine Robb Whyte to Edith Robb, 1937

MOUNT ASSINIBOINE, SEPTEMBER SNOW

Peter and Catharine Whyte chose the Assiniboine area for their 1937 September sketching trip. Catharine's daily letters to her mother in Boston provide a play-by-play account of their activities. They started out in ideal conditions, and the successful first day of perfect sketching conditions was followed by another, and another, but soon they found themselves subject to the temperamental weather of the Assiniboine. She writes:

"Tuesday seemed to be blowing up something. Great clouds and mist in the valleys in the morning. Very beautiful effects… but by afternoon there were almost too many clouds… It started snowing in the evening and there was about four inches when we went to bed. By next morning, Wednesday, it was still snowing, a good ten inches on the ground and it snowed all day. About five we measured 15 inches which is quite a fall. The next morning, Pete could hardly wait to get out and paint only he had to stand on cabin porches as too much snow was falling and got all over the palette and canvas… I painted out the door in the A.M. and out the window in the P.M. Pete thought it was the best day we had had for painting."[42]

The Whytes stayed for another week, capturing the various effects of the weather in the Assiniboine area.

TRAIL INFO

Trail information: Assiniboine via Wonder Pass
Type of hike: Overnight backpack
Best time to go: January through April, or summer
Trailhead: The Mount Shark parking lot on the Smith-Dorrien/Spray Lake trail out of Canmore
Distance: 25.6 km, plus a 3.6 km return side trip to Marvel Lake
Elevation gain: 685 m
Degree of difficulty: Moderate to difficult
Hiking time: Allow 3 days
Topo map: 82 J/13, 82 J/14
Route: The trail leads away from the Mount Shark parking lot to the Palliser Pass junction at 6.2 km. Cross the upper Spray River and Bryant Creek, and ascend the Bryant Creek Valley. Pass the Big Springs campground at 9.7 km and the junction to Owl Lake at 12.1 km. You will reach the Bryant Creek Warden Cabin and the junction for Wonder Pass at 14.3 km. Just before the junction to Marvel Lake you will pass another campground. The side trip to Marvel Lake begins here and adds 3.6 km return to the trip. To reach the lake, take the left junction across Bryant Creek. You will reach the lakeshore in 1.2 km. Return to the main trail and continue to Wonder Pass at 23.8 km. The trail continues up past several junctions (keep to the main trail) and you will reach Magog Lake at the foot of Mount Assiniboine at 25.9 km.

Belmore Browne
Rainy Day at Marvel Lake, 1934
oil on canvas, Glenbow Collection

A.C. Leighton painting at Assiniboine, date unknown

"TWO THINGS HAVE GOT ON MY NERVES —

ONE THE ROAR AND HISSING AND POUNDING ALL

NIGHT LONG OF A TREMENDOUS WATERFALL

THAT I AM NEAR, THE OTHER THE ALIGHTING OF

SNOWFLAKES ON MY BOTTOM WHEN IT IS

BARED ONCE A DAY. PERHAPS THIS IS THE

POETRY OF CAMPING OUT."

— John Singer Sargent to his cousin Mary, 1916

John Singer Sargent
Lake O'Hara, September, 1916, 1916
oil on canvas, Fogg Art Collection

I got to the beautiful Lake O'Hara

lying in a rainbow sleep,

under the steeps of Mount Lefroy

and the waterfalls of Oesa.

And there I realized some

of the blessedness

of mortals…

I looked at the emerald

and violet of her colour. It is

emerald and malachite, and jade,

and rainbow green, and mermaids eyes…

These are some of the people

who stand about O'Hara:

Lefroy, Victoria, Huber,

Wiwaxy, Cathedral, Odaray…

I have memories

of the clearest crystal

mountain days imaginable,

when we fortunates in the height

seemed to be sky people

living in light alone…

—J.E.H. MacDonald in *Canadian Bookman*, 1924

LAKE O'HARA

The mecca of the mountains, and without a doubt the area of the western Rockies most often painted, is Lake O'Hara, perched on the edge of the Continental Divide, just across the Alberta border into British Columbia. The remarkable variety of mountainscape that the Lake O'Hara area contains has resulted in a 100-year history of artwork created by artists and photographers.

The persistent appeal of this region since the turn of the century is due in part to its long history of relatively easy access. The Lake O'Hara trail system is thought to be based on old Stoney and Kootenay Indian trade trails which were later used by railway surveyors and alpinists. James Joseph McArthur conducted an 1892 survey for the Dominion of Canada, and his detailed and vivid descriptions led Colonel Robert O'Hara of the British Army, to whom the area owes its name, to visit the region. Colonel O'Hara's fascination with the endless variety of the area drew him back to explore repeatedly. Perhaps he was drawn by McArthur's compelling description:

"...a beautiful piece of park-like country...the view on all sides one of indescribable grandeur...I counted sixteen Alpine Lakes, one of which is more strikingly beautiful than any other I have ever seen...a clear blue face...dotted with miniature icebergs...."[43]

The area was mapped by mountaineer Samuel Allen in 1894, and Lake O'Hara's reputation as a beauty spot spread quickly. In 1920, the CPR built a lodge at the lakeshore as part of its rapidly developing accommodation program in the Rockies. The elite CPR hotels at Lake Louise and Banff were a great success, and with tourists becoming more adventurous and looking further up the mountains for their enjoyment, the CPR developed Lake O'Hara into a comfortable lodge with adjacent cabins. These were used as a painting base by artists who came by pack horse up the Cataract Brook valley from Hector Station (at Wapta Lake) on the CPR line.

LAKE O'HARA, SEPTEMBER, 1916

Boston portrait painter John Singer Sargent visited Lake O'Hara in 1916 with Earl Gammon, superintendent of the Brewster Company, as his outfitter. At the time, Sargent was one of the most famous painters in the United States, and his attention to Lake O'Hara immediately threw a spotlight on the region. His canvas of the lake became a popular work, and drew an untold number of eastern travellers, particularly Bostonians, to the Rockies and Lake O'Hara, and inspired other artists to take sketching trips to the mountains. The vantage point from which Sargent painted this work is now known as "Sargent's Point," and lies a few hundred metres down the west-bound path around Lake O'Hara, near the warden's cabin.

While at O'Hara, Sargent wrote to his cousin Mary, with whom he was quite close. In these letters he complained constantly about the conditions of camping out, yet conveyed that he was really enjoying himself. He wrote to her on August 30, 1916:

"As I told you in my first or my last [letter] it was raining and snowing, my tent flooded, mushrooms sprouting in my boots, porcupines taking shelter in my clothes, canned food always fried in a black frying pan getting on my nerves, and a fine waterfall which is the attraction of the place pounding and thundering all night. I stood it three weeks and yesterday came away with a repulsive picture. Now the weather has changed for the better and I am off again to try the simple life (ach pfui) in tents at the top of another valley, this time with a gridiron instead of a frying pan and a perforated Indian rubber mat to stand on. It takes time to learn how to be really happy."[44]

Five works resulted from the trip: Lake O'Hara, September, 1916; A Tent Inside (Canadian Rockies); Tents at Lake O'Hara; View of Mountains; and Yoho Falls, Canadian Rocky Mountains (the latter four are not illustrated).

J.W.G. (Jock) Macdonald
Mount Lefroy, Lake O'Hara, 1944
oil on canvas, The University of British Columbia,
Morris and Helen Belkin Art Gallery

"YOU TAKE A PENCIL, YOU ARE IN A QUIET PLACE, YOU PUT THE PENCIL ON THE PAPER AND YOU SIT THERE UNTIL YOUR HAND MOVES OF ITS OWN ACCORD. YOU DO THAT EVERY DAY. YOU KEEP DOING IT. IT WILL HAPPEN WITHOUT ANY EFFORT ON YOUR PART."

— Artist Marion Nicoll describing Jock Macdonald's instructions for automatic drawing, 1946

MOUNT LEFROY, LAKE O'HARA

James Williamson Galloway (Jock) Macdonald's career spanned some 35 years and reached from the east to the west coast of Canada. He was born in Scotland, where he went on to study at the Edinburgh College of Art, and later to work at a prominent textile design firm. He came to Canada in 1926 to teach at the Vancouver School of Decorative and Applied Arts. There he met Fred Varley, a founding member of the Group of Seven, who took him sketching into the British Columbia mountains, and stimulated Macdonald's interest in landscape painting. This new subject of landscape forced a transition from Macdonald's preferred media of watercolour and tempera, to explorations in linoleum block printing, sculpture, and oil. He had found that watercolour and tempera, were not strong enough to capture his particular vision of the scenery.

Macdonald also began to explore new means of spiritual expression, including theosophical symbolism and transcendentalism. He eventually came to feel that it was "the creative artist's duty to convey new reflection about life which the masses have not yet become aware of...."[45]

In 1940, Lawren Harris moved to Vancouver, where Macdonald was working at the Technical High School "in order to exist,"[46] and suffering from poor health. The arrival of Harris, whose work he appreciated, whose writings inspired him, and whose philosophical beliefs he shared, was refreshing and encouraging. They spent the summer of 1941 painting in the Rockies, and Macdonald would return there on his own in 1942 and 1943.

In 1945, Macdonald taught at the Banff School of Fine Arts, exploring with his students the practice of automatic drawing, which he had been exposed to by British psychiatrist Dr. Grace Pailthorpe in Vancouver. This technique is used by artists to tap the subconscious mind by allowing the hand and brush to move freely on the work surface.

Macdonald also taught in Calgary, Toronto, and Victoria, and was a member of the group known as Painters Eleven. He accepted several teaching fellowships abroad, and began to receive formal recognition for his efforts in the late 1950s. His contributions to abstract painting in Canada equal his impact as a teacher, and he was to continue both activities until his death in 1960.

J.E.H. MacDonald
Cathedral Peak and Lake O'Hara, 1927
oil on panel, McMichael Canadian Art Collection

"IF THERE IS TRULY A HEAVEN, THEN I WANT

A BERTH IN THE LAKE O'HARA REGION OF THE

ROCKY MOUNTAINS."

— J.E.H. MacDonald diaries,
    National Archives of Canada, 1926

CATHEDRAL PEAK AND LAKE O'HARA

J.E.H. MacDonald was a leading member of the Group of Seven and champion of a school of unique Canadian art. He was also a poet, whose writings played a critical role in his painting. He believed that the two arts were complementary, and the painter would improve his work if he were also a poet. Each was an exercise in careful economy — economy of words, of colour, of content, and of structure. MacDonald's economy was conditioned by his training in Art Nouveau design principles which helped him to tame the tangled qualities of nature into readable rhythms and patterns. Elements of this design training can be seen in much of his painting.

MacDonald travelled west to Yoho National Park's Lake O'Hara region for the first time in the fall of 1924. He was deeply impressed with what he found:

"…there were grey cold days when one heard echoes of chaos and cold nights on the upper slopes and the spirit of desolation wafted coldly about the rock-slides, and found the sight of even a little old dried horse dung a consolation and assurance. On such days, and often in the calm and still weather, one felt that the mountains are not completed. The builders are still at work. Stones come rolling and jumping from the upper scaffolding and often from the chasms one hears the thunderings as the gods of the mountains change their plans. In these great places all the functions of Nature are on a big scale and the material workings of the frost and wind and rain are clear to us."[47]

His annual autumn trips were always timed to coincide with the height of the larches. He kept detailed diaries of each of his trips west. His entries convey his eye for colour, the effects of light and shadow and pattern, and are interspersed with quotations from philosophy that he found worthy of noting, notes regarding each day's sketching, and his own prolific poems. He writes on September 17, 1930:

"Clear sun on lake and mountains…such delicacy of shadow on Lefroy and Lake Odaray and such beauty of colour in lake. The lighter poem of wind breaking, the vividness of blue green where sun touches smooth water and blending of smooth water in light from dark blue-green to fullness of green near foreground. Try painting for this effect."[48]

J.E.H. MacDonald
Wiwaxy Peaks, Lake O'Hara, 1926
oil on medium weight card, McMichael Canadian Art Collection

WIWAXY PEAKS, LAKE O'HARA

Sometime between 1924 and 1926,[49] Peter Whyte met J.E.H. MacDonald and began to accompany him on his painting hikes. MacDonald had confided to Sid Graves, then host of Lake O'Hara Lodge, that he was a bit nervous about bears and being out in the mountains alone. In the 1920s, the well-defined trails that now traverse O'Hara were rough goat paths. Rock scrambling and bushwhacking were often the means of access to the area's nooks and crannies. MacDonald and Whyte took to each other immediately, and became regular sketching companions for the remainder of MacDonald's visits to the Rockies. Peter wrote to Catharine in 1928:

"There is an artist here from Toronto, Mr. J.E.H. MacDonald... He is a lovable old Scotchman with red hair, a remarkably fine painter. We get along fine together and tramp and paint together all day. He is so sincere and honest about things, and has a keen sense of humour... Yesterday and the day before, Mr. MacDonald and myself walked up towards Opabin Pass a few miles, taking our lunches along, and spent the days sketching and observing. The high valleys have such nice soft carpets of moss and grass that after eating lunch we sprawl out on the ground and rest until we know we shouldn't waste anymore time but back to the sketch box again."[50]

In 1930, MacDonald would make his last trip to O'Hara and would spend almost the entire trip sketching with the Whytes. His lengthy diary from that trip contains some interesting observations about the weather, now showing signs of the drought conditions of the Depression:

"In the mountains west of Banff, the haze continues. It hasn't the quick recessive quality of smoke haze being obviously due to the heat. Water is low, in places dry, but the foliage and fields are green as at home. Little snow or ice visible yet. Effects tame, would not be approved of by L.S.H. [Lawren Harris], but radiant weather."[51]

Upon his return to Toronto in late September after the 1930 visit to O'Hara, MacDonald wrote sentimental and reminiscent letters to the Whytes:

"The mountains are a dream now. I haven't quite awakened from it and hope you are still enjoying the full beauty of it. And very beautiful it was to come through that native Bow Valley of yours. Colour and subjects galore and galumptious." He goes on, awakening slowly from his dream: *"But what have these things to do with office and routine and curriculum and courses and other remnants of the Fall of Man."[52]*

By 1930, MacDonald's responsibilities as a teacher were affecting his already poor health (he had suffered a major stroke in 1917), and his plans for another trip to O'Hara were uncertain. He writes to Peter Whyte in June of 1931:

"At present the outlook is poor as I am laid up with something, due apparently to too much Art School. But here's hoping. Kindest regards to the good wife and salutations to the mountains."[53]

His health required a trip of gentler conditions than September in a Canadian Rockies log cabin would offer, and MacDonald went to Barbados that year. He would not return to the West, and died in Toronto in 1932. Catharine Whyte later said of him:

"Pete knew him so well and told me so much about him. I can hardly believe I was only there one summer when he was there; he made such a strong impression on me. He used to get up early and throw little pebbles at our cabin and they'd run down the roof and wake us up because he wanted to get started early when he was sketching. It didn't matter how cold it was, he'd still go."[54]

J.E.H. MacDonald
Lake O'Hara with Snow, undated
oil on panel, Glenbow Collection

"TO BE A TRAINSMAN AND CALL OUT "LAKE LOUISE."

THIS IS SOMETHING IN THE WAY OF SPECIALTIES, AND FEW THERE BE THAT

FIND IT. LAKE LOUISE SHOULD BE ANNOUNCED ON A RADIO RECORD BY

JOHN MACCORMICK OR SOME SUCH ANGEL. BUT LAKE O'HARA

HAS TO BE APPROACHED IN MORE REVERENT STEPS. "MY GENTLE HARP"

ON THE PIPE ORGAN WITH A SORT OF NATURE MASS WRITTEN BY W.B. YEATS."

— J.E.H. MacDonald diaries, National Archives of Canada, 1930

"HE ALWAYS CARRIED A HEAVY ULSTER FOLDED

OVER HIS ARM AND A COLLAPSIBLE UMBRELLA WHICH

HE STUCK INTO THE GROUND. HE SAT ON A ROCK ON

HIS ULSTER, WITH HIS NOSE RUNNING ALL THE TIME,

MADE TEA IN A PAIL WHICH HE CACHED AT OESA

AND OPABIN… WITH STUBBY BRUSHES WORN DOWN

TO THE METAL."

— Dr. George K.K.(Tommy) Link, visitor to Lake O'Hara
and friend of J.E.H. MacDonald, before 1979

LAKE O'HARA WITH SNOW

Lake O'Hara with Snow depicts the bases of Mounts Victoria
and Lefroy, across the lake striped with new snow, their rocks
slick and wet, on one of those fall days when you wake up in
your mountain tent with everything thoroughly soaked. The
vertical, repeating brushwork that runs throughout the
painting, conveys the quality of the water in the lake, cold
and still, but as yet unfrozen, and captures the wetness
caused by snow rather than rain.

COLOURS BY GRASSI

Hikers at O'Hara, today, enjoy the marvelous
trails built by Lawrence Grassi, who became
warden at Lake O'Hara in 1956. He then helped
the Lake O'Hara Trails Club finish the work it
had begun by completing the trail to Lake
Oesa. Grassi was already famous for his trail
work in Banff, Kananaskis, Skoki, and Lake
Louise, because his trails are a marvel of
engineering, and a delight to hike. Huge, flat
slabs of rock make ascending the jumbled flank
of Mount Huber easy on your feet, and the
pinks and blues of the Gog quartzite, siltstone,
sandstone, and shale, common to the region,
make colourful steps. These metamorphic rocks
paint the trails of O'Hara with pinks, blues,
greens, and whites, and can be seen in many
paintings of the region, particularly those of
Carl Rungius. Fossilized worm burrows criss-cross
the weathered surfaces, and ripple marks
parallel each other, creating a mosaic of texture
underfoot. The colour of the rock in this area of
the mountains is due to the high iron content,
and changes in the weather and light conditions
all affect the palette. The Seven Sisters Falls, as
they cascade into Lake O'Hara, create a vivid
kaleidoscope of bouncing and blending colour,
as light reflects off wet rock, passes through
water and highlights spray.

Carl Rungius
Mountain Lake (Lake O'Hara), undated
oil on canvas, Glenbow Collection

"LAKE O'HARA IS MORE THAN JUST A LAKE. IT IS THE

GENTLE TRAIL THAT CIRCLES THE LAKE. IT IS… STEEP SWITCHBACKS

THAT LEAD UP TO GRAND VIEWS AT WIWAXY GAP…

THE ELEGANT… STONE WALKWAY PAST RUMBLING WATERFALLS AND…

TINY LAKELETS TO LAKE OESA… COVERED IN ICE WELL INTO THE SUMMER…

THE HIGH ALPINE ROUTE FROM OESA… TO OPABIN PASS,

A GLACIER-SHROUDED SHOULDER FROM WHICH MOUNTAINEERS MAKE

THEIR WAY DOWN TO EAGLE'S AERIES AND UP TO WENKCHEMNA

PASS AND MORAINE LAKE IN BANFF NATIONAL PARK."

— R.W. Sandford in *Yoho: A History and Celebration*, 1993

Catharine Robb Whyte
In the High Country, Wiwaxy Peak, 1937
oil on canvas board, Whyte Museum of the Canadian Rockies

J.W.G. (Jock) Macdonald
Lake McArthur, 1941
oil on board
Collection of Don and Shirley Grace

"I STILL DO MY UTMOST TO KEEP PAINTING —
AT LEAST SOMETHING EVERY WEEK. I AM STILL DOING
LANDSCAPES BUT FIND MY SEMI-ABSTRACTS, OR WHAT
I CALL 'MODALITIES,' A DEEPER VALUE TO ME...
FOR ME, ABSTRACT AND SEMI-ABSTRACT CREATIONS
ARE THE STATEMENTS OF THE NEW AND AWAKENING
CONSCIOUSNESS."

— Jock Macdonald to H.O. McCurry, 1943

LAKE MCARTHUR, YOHO PARK

A short, steep, 3.5 kilometre hike away from Lake O'Hara, nestled against the foot of Mount Biddle, and watched over by Mount Schäffer and Park Mountain, lies Lake McArthur. The trail up to the site travels past shallow Schäffer Lake and on through a jungle of tumbled boulders. This may be the lake that J.J. McArthur mentioned as having been more beautiful than any he had ever seen, its blue being a deeper blue than most glacial-fed lakes, and its face dotted with ice floes in the spring.

Lake McArthur captures perfectly the deep blue of the lake's waters and the aged patina of the surrounding mountains. The churning brushwork, the rendering of the patterns of rock, the surface of the snow, and the movement in the sky are intuitive and unrestricted.

The Rocky Mountains and nature provided Jock Macdonald with continuity, inspiration, and solace from the frustration that lack of critical acclaim and overwork brought him. His trips to the Rockies in 1941, 1942, and 1943, were great sources of sustenance, and while he worked primarily in an abstract vein subsequent to these trips, his work was always based on natural subjects. He sought his personal spiritual fulfillment in the natural world, continually returning to the elements and creative forces of nature.

After suffering a heart attack in November of 1960 and just prior to his death that Christmas season, he contemplated the day and wrote from his hospital bed:

"A beautiful morning of life giving sunshine. The happiness, the only happiness there is, is in the constant seeking for understanding of the highest spiritual consciousness."[55]

TRAIL INFO

Trail information: Lake McArthur
Type of hike: Day hike from Lake O'Hara
Best time to go: Late August or early September
Trailhead: At the Lake O'Hara warden's cabin
Distance: 3.5 km
Elevation gain: 395 m
Degree of difficulty: Moderate
Hiking time: Allow the better part of a day to explore the region
Topo map: 82 N/8
Route: From the warden's cabin, follow the signed trail to Schäffer Lake. At the junction, stay left to McArthur Lake. You will begin to climb shortly after you pass Schäffer Lake. Watch for the wonderful views to Cathedral Mountain from the cliff traverse at 2.8 km. You will reach the lakeshore at 3.5 km.

"NATURE IS STILL MY MEDIUM FOR STUDY AND I

BELIEVE AS DEFINITELY AS EVER THAT THERE CAN BE NO

ART WITH AESTHETIC VALUES WHICH HAS NO

CONTACT WITH NATURE."

— Jock Macdonald to H.O. McCurry, 1939

J.E.H. MacDonald
Lake McArthur, Yoho Park, 1924
oil on cardboard, National Gallery of Canada

Arthur Lismer
Cathedral Mountain, 1928
oil on canvas, Montreal Museum of Fine Arts

"...THIS CATHEDRAL MOUNTAIN TO ME WAS LIKE A GREAT GOTHIC STRUCTURE. IT WAS AN AMAZING THING. WE WERE UP ABOUT 6 TO 7000 FEET, I SUPPOSE, AND FROM EVERY ANGLE AND IN A VAST TERRITORY LIKE THIS YOU HAD TO TALK TO YOUR PREY, AS IT WERE, TO FIND A WAY OF GETTING AT IT... THERE WERE BUTTRESSES AND THE PILLARS, TOWERS AND SUPPORTING WEIGHTS LIKE A VAST PIECE OF ARCHITECTURE...."

— Arthur Lismer in a letter to J. Russell Harper, undated

CATHEDRAL MOUNTAIN

Cathedral Mountain, at 3189 metres, is an imposing peak which guards the entrance to Lake O'Hara. Tiny Teacup Lake at the top has been responsible for a great deal of trouble for the CPR tracks down below. The glacier on the lake intermittently dams the waters, and the dam occasionally bursts, flooding the tracks below.

In 1928, Arthur Lismer followed the lead of Lawren Harris and A.Y. Jackson, and went west to the Rockies to paint. Members of the Group were looking for new subjects, and were exploring the vast regions of Canada from the Skeena River to Pangnirtung. Lismer visited the Lake Louise and Lake O'Hara regions, signing the registration book at Lake O'Hara Lodge on August 20, 1928, and with wife Esther and young daughter Marjorie, he settled into cabin three. He began to paint from Opabin Plateau above Lake O'Hara, looking back towards Cathedral Mountain. He later remembered the mountain's impact:

"We'd been painting in Georgian Bay and Algonquin Park where all the horizons were straight and the trees stuck up [but] this is the kind of adoration that you look up and find the glory — the clouds coming to it... You had a feeling of omniscience about the place and then you looked up to the top of these mountains. Well the idea was to reduce these forms away from the usual topographical photography that you see in brochures and so on and try to get some kind of design out of it. And you'd begin to ...see a rhythm that united sky and land...it was very challenging...you can't reproduce a mountain on a small sketch and size... Cathedral Mountain is a memory. Looking down at a little green lake surrounded by the spruce and pine and looking up and seeing this thing soaring into the clouds which took up the rhythm and fetched it into an almighty paean of praise...."[56]

Lismer's composition looks across Lake O'Hara from Opabin Plateau, high above the valley floor. This was a popular sketching spot for many artists, likely due to the panoramic views that include Cathedral Mountain, the Wiwaxy Peaks, Mount Huber, and the gemstone colours of Lake O'Hara below.

J.E.H. MacDonald
Clearing Weather, Sherbrooke Lake, Above Wapta Lake, c.1928 or 1929
oil on cardboard, National Gallery of Canada

> "TO PAINT FROM NATURE IS TO REALIZE ONE'S SENSATIONS, NOT TO COPY WHAT IS BEFORE ONE."

— J.E.H. MacDonald papers, National Archives of Canada, 1929

THE YOHO VALLEY

CLEARING WEATHER, SHERBROOKE LAKE, ABOVE WAPTA LAKE

The Sherbrooke Valley was named by surveyor J.J. McArthur for the Quebec town of Sherbrooke. The lake is a short distance away from Lake O'Hara and one of the few places outside of O'Hara that J.E.H. MacDonald is known to have sketched. This small oil, which looks north across the lake and up the Sherbrooke Valley, shows Mount Ogden in rolling green immediately rising from the opposite bank, with the upcurved peak of Mount Niles towering behind. On the right, Mount Daly and the edge of the Daly Glacier show above the lower flanks of Paget Peak. The foreground of the sketch has an almost neo-impressionist feel — short, broad strokes of colour depict the rocky shoreline of the lake, interspersed with squarish puddles here and there and touches of fall colour.

When J.E.H. MacDonald came to the Rocky Mountains and began to sketch in Yoho National Park, he was consumed by a patriotic love of the Canadian landscape that grew stronger with each year that he returned. In the 1924 manuscript titled "A Glimpse of the West," he professed his love for the Rockies, and wished that:

"If I could, I would send every Canadian east of Sault-Saint Marie to the West as a post-graduate course in patriotism, with an exchange of privileges if the westerners wanted it. A man would have to have the soul of a buffalo not to be broadened by the sight of those wide prairies, and the mountains should hold and deepen the broadening."[57]

The Rockies came to be MacDonald's yearly release from the pressures of teaching, and his writings about them reflect his deepening attachment to Yoho Park and his love for the scenery of the area. Each year at the end of the 3330 kilometre train trip from Toronto to the Rockies, he would disembark at Wapta Station on the CPR line in Yoho National Park and prepare for the trip by pack horse into Lake O'Hara:

"Here was blue Wapta Lake, or is it malachite or emerald or rainbow green, many are the terms people use. Let any of them conjure up the paint colour your mental eye can picture. You cannot overdo it. Rainbow green seems to me the best. It has a soft quality of light and change and variation of intensity which comes nearest to the feeling of the lake colour."[58]

Sherbrooke Lake is the site of one of the famous grizzly attacks in the Canadian Rockies which involved photographer Nicholas Morant and Swiss guide Christian Häsler, who were surveying the lake as a possible CPR teahouse site in 1939. The attack was vicious and both men nearly lost their lives. It is an unsettling story to recall while on the shores of this tranquil lake, but a cautionary reminder of the constant presence of wildlife in the Rockies.

Lawren Harris
Glaciers, Rocky Mountains, 1930
oil on card, London Regional Art and Historical Museums

"ALWAYS IT SEEKS ORDER, AN INEVITABLE STRUCTURE, A WEAVING OF ALL PARTS INTO A UNITY BEYOND QUESTIONING. SO AGE AFTER AGE, ART GIVES US ASSURANCE OF THAT WHICH IS AGELESS, FOREVER NEW, POSITIVE AND GLORIOUS…. ART IS MAN'S ECSTASY."

— Lawren Harris in *Canadian Comment on Current Events*, 1933

GLACIERS, ROCKY MOUNTAINS

"Yoho National Park takes its name from a Cree expression of awe and wonder. The Yoho and Little Yoho valleys contain a concentration of the park's wonders: powerful and picturesque waterfalls, glacier-clad peaks, and pockets of alpine meadow."[59]

Yoho's wonders are numerous and include Takakkaw and Twin Falls, the Wapta Icefield, the Whaleback, and Yoho Glacier.

Lawren Harris's explorations of the area took him into Yoho's heart, and his work *Glaciers, Rocky Mountains,* depicts one of the outstanding vistas of the region.

The Waterfall Valley is known in particular for solitude and an abundance of wildlife. This is due to the fact that the trail is currently unmaintained, and that many hikers visit the region with a trip to Twin Falls in mind. Mont des Poilus is an outstanding peak, dominating the view in every direction, and only hinting at the vast icefields that lie beyond.

TRAIL INFO

Trail information: Mont des Poilus – Waterfall Valley - Yoho National Park
Type of hike: Unmaintained spur trail – overnight backpack
Best time to go: Summer
Trailhead: Takakkaw Falls parking lot
Distance: 12.7 km
Elevation gain: 215 m
Degree of difficulty: Moderate
Hiking time: Allow 2 days
Topo map: 82 N/7, 82 N/8, 82 N/9, 82 N/10
Route: Start at the Takakkaw Falls parking lot and follow the trail and the signs to Twin Falls at 8.1 km. Watch the views along this trail as it takes you past Twin Falls and into the Whaleback area. Continue on the Whaleback trail which switchbacks upwards to a crossing via a suspension bridge over Twin Falls Creek near the lip of Twin Falls. Watch for an unmarked trail junction at 10.9 km. This unmaintained trail takes you to Mont des Poilus Meadows at 12.7 km. Return the way you came, or follow the Whaleback trail back out to a junction with the Little Yoho Valley trail (go left) which connects with the Yoho Valley main trail and heads back to the Takakkaw Falls parking lot.

ISOLATION PEAK ISOLATED

The titles of the drawings and paintings depicting the mountains shown in *Glaciers, Rocky Mountains,* by Lawren Harris, have been the cause of some geographical confusion. The canvas known as *Isolation Peak,* which depicts this same place, is responsible for the confusion. As the work is a well-known canvas, untitled preliminary works showing various renditions of the same scene have come to be known as sketches or drawings for *Isolation Peak*.

There is, in fact, no mountain named Isolation Peak in the Canadian Rockies. There is a mountain named Isolated Peak, which happens to lie quite near the mountains that Harris has painted, adding to the confusion. In all of these works, Harris's composition depicts Mont des Poilus and Arête Peaks, Yoho National Park, British Columbia, in the greater Wapta Icefield.

Mont des Poilus was named to commemorate the hundreds of young French privates lost in the First World War, and is the triangular, dominating peak in Harris's scene. Arête Peak is the curving rock formation lying on Mont des Poilus's flank. Yoho Peak slopes upwards on the right and the Wapta Icefield and Glacier des Poilus lie to the left and right respectively. Harris worked looking northeast towards the icefield from the Waterfall Valley below Mont des Poilus, and in fact he would have been able to view the mountain Isolated Peak (which looks nothing like any of Harris's images) by looking back over his shoulder to the south.

The reason for the confusion surrounding the name is unclear. Inscriptions by Harris on the works do not indicate how the title came to be established. One work carries the title *Isolation Peak above Yoho Valley, Rocky Mountains* (not illustrated), which gives credence to the argument that the title is evocative. Perhaps Harris heard the name Isolated Peak while in the area and logically applied it to this work, as Mont des Poilus is very isolated indeed, rising sharply out of the middle of a sheet of ice. If the title was intended to be evocative rather than literal, it is an odd coincidence that a mountain called Isolated Peak is found so close by.

As titles certainly do not a work of art make, the confusion is of little consequence to our enjoyment of the painting. For those interested in hiking to the actual place Harris depicted, however, it matters, so set your sights on Mont des Poilus, and the Whaleback trail in Yoho's Waterfall Valley.

Lawren Harris
Isolation Peak, Rocky Mountains, 1930
oil on canvas, Hart House Permanent Collection

Lawren Harris
Emerald Lake, c.1924
oil on panel, McMichael Canadian Art Collection

"...A GEM OF PERFECT BEAUTY, ITS COLOURING
MARVELOUSLY RICH AND VIVID, AND CONSTANTLY
CHANGING UNDER THE SHIFTING LIGHTS AND
SHADES."

— Sir James Outram, alpinist, c.1880s

EMERALD LAKE

EMERALD LAKE

Justly named for its glimmering jewel-toned greens, Emerald Lake was one of the early destinations for artists visiting the Rockies, as the Emerald Lake Lodge on its shore was built in 1902 by the CPR. Lawren Harris visited Emerald Lake in 1924 on his first trip to the Canadian Rockies, which would also take him to Jasper where he would meet A.Y. Jackson for an extended painting trip into the backcountry. Harris's depictions of Emerald Lake represent his work before the mountains had taken hold of him:

"When I first saw the mountains, travelled through them, I was discouraged. Nowhere did they measure up to the advertising folders, or to the conceptions these had formed in the mind's eye." But as he warmed to them, and began to explore their possibilities: *"I found a power and a majesty and a wealth of experience at nature's summit which no travel-folder ever expressed."*[60]

TRAIL INFO

Trail information: Emerald Lake
Type of hike: Pleasant lakeshore stroll
Best time to go: September
Trailhead: Emerald Lake parking lot
Distance: 5 km
Elevation gain: 10 m
Degree of difficulty: Very easy
Hiking time: Allow 1 1/2 hrs
Topo map: 82 N/7
Route: You can follow the trail around Emerald Lake clockwise or counter-clockwise, but if you hike clockwise the views are better. At about 600 m, your view will approximate Harris's composition. You will pass two junctions, the first at 1.4 km marks the trail to Yoho Pass, and the second at 3.9 km leads to Burgess Pass. Spend some time watching the colours of the lake change, they truly are a remarkable collection of greens. If you have time, a steep 5.3 km side trip to Hamilton Lake and Falls provides superb views down to Emerald Lake cradled 833 m below, and even finer views of the peaks in the valley beyond. Mount Wapta, Mount Field, Cathedral Mountain, and the Goodsirs, rise prominently into view through the trees.

"THE MOUNTAINS, THE PEAKS, THE GLACIERS,

THAT'S WHERE I WANT TO BE AND WHAT I WANT TO PAINT."

— A.C. Leighton in *A.C. Leighton and the Canadian Rockies,* c.1930s

A.C. Leighton
Floe Lake, Marble Canyon, 1930
watercolour on paper, Glenbow Collection

"THE ROCKWALL IS AMONGST THE CREAM OF THE CLASSIC HIKES — A REMARKABLE OUTING THAT EPITOMIZES THE SPECTACULAR LANDSCAPE OF THE ROCKIES. PEAK, PASS, AND PRECIPICE; MEADOW AND STREAM; GLACIER AND TARN — THE ROCKWALL WEAVES THESE QUINTESSENTIAL ELEMENTS INTO ONE OF THE MOST REWARDING BACKPACKING EXCURSIONS IN THE RANGE."

– Graeme Pole in *Classic Hikes in the Canadian Rockies*, 1994

FLOE LAKE, MARBLE CANYON

Located off the Banff-Radium Highway in Kootenay National Park, the vast formation known as the Rockwall is aptly named, running for 40 seemingly impenetrable kilometres and standing 500 metres high. Floe Lake, which lies below, dotted with discarded bits of the persistent glacier clinging above her, captured the attention of English-born A.C. Leighton in 1930.

In 1929, Leighton became the head of the art department of the Provincial Institute of Technology and Art, and set up permanent residence in Alberta. He undertook painting expeditions as often as the pressures of work and his declining health permitted, and packed into the mountains, where, for two to three weeks at a time, and often in the dead of winter, he would spend hours looking, carefully selecting a scene, making thumbnail sketches, and watching the light change before he would begin a picture. He became increasingly attracted to the more remote locations in the Rockies, looking for sites above the tree line and shunning the comforts of the lodges that so many artists chose as bases for their painting trips: "The mountains, the peaks, the glaciers, that's where I want to be and what I want to paint."[61]

Floe Lake, Marble Canyon, is a descriptive painting, even-toned, and very understated. The surface of the Rockwall is worked in thin washes of seamless watercolour based on meticulous drawing of the cliffs and chutes of the rock face and the lake — a perfect stage view. The addition of twisted, inky, calligraphic trees in the foreground is a pure Leighton device, anchoring the perspective of the work by their darker tone and placement. This device is akin to Tom Thomson's "blasted pine" device, and served Leighton well, often appearing in his Rocky Mountain works.

The trail to Floe Lake travels through a mature forest of lodgepole pine and spruce swept by numerous avalanche paths, allowing hints of the looming Rockwall as you advance up the trail. The Floe Lake valley is beautiful and well worth an overnight stay to enjoy the changing nature of the Rockwall face that so attracted Leighton. In summer, the valley floor fills with wildflowers of every description, and in fall, the larch needles turn to threads of saffron, spicing the early snows with delicate colour. Take time to watch the shadows move across the Rockwall, and look for the moment when they echo those in the painting.

TRAIL INFO

Trail information: Floe Lake, Marble Canyon
Type of hike: Day hike or overnight backpack
Distance: 10.5 km
Trailhead: Drive the Banff-Radium Highway to the Floe Lake trail parking area, 22.4 km south of the British Columbia /Alberta border
Elevation gain: 730 m
Topo map: 82 N/1
Degree of difficulty: Moderate
Route: Follow the dirt access road for 400 m to the bridged crossing of the Vermilion River. The trail begins here. At 1.7 km you will cross Floe Creek, and the moderate uphill climb begins. At 5.7 km there are about 300 m of steep switchbacks, followed by 2 km of steep switchbacks at 8 km. The trail levels out at 10.1 km, and another 400 m brings you to Floe Lake at 10.5 km. Once you are in the Floe Lake area proper, a number of additional hiking trails beckon. Tumbling Pass and the trail to Tumbling Glacier lead off to the northwest, following the unending cliffs of The Rockwall. You can continue on this trail past Wolverine Pass, to Rockwall Pass, along Helmut Creek, and back out to the highway via Ochre Creek and the Paintpots.

A.C. Leighton sketching on the Bow River, c.1935

"YOU HAVE TO KEEP PAINTING OUTDOORS;

IF YOU PAINT OUTDOOR SCENES IN

THE STUDIO YOUR COLOUR INVARIABLY

GETS TOO WARM, TOO HOT.

ONLY IF YOU PAINT OUTDOORS

DO YOU SEE THE COOL SILVERY TONES

THAT ARE THE TRUE COLOURS

OF NATURE."

— Carl Rungius to wildlife artist Clarence Tillenius,
c.1930-40

Carl Rungius
Crowfoot Glacier, undated
oil on canvas, Glenbow Collection

"SOME PEOPLE MAKE ONLY HALF THE TRIP…

RETURNING THE WAY THEY CAME. YET, THE FULLEST

AND MOST REWARDING TRIP IS TO TRAVEL THE

ROUTE IN ITS ENTIRETY, MOVING AT A LEISURELY

PACE AND TAKING TIME TO EXPLORE SOME OF THE

SCENIC TRAILS THAT WANDER OFF THROUGH

SUBALPINE FOREST AND FLOWERED ALPINE TUNDRA."

–Brian Patton in *Parkways of the Canadian Rockies*, 1982

CROWFOOT GLACIER

The spectacular drive along the Icefields Parkway takes you past more than 100 glaciers and through alpine landscape covered in wildflowers, past winding rivers that erode their way through broad valleys and threads of waterfalls that cascade down vertical cliffs. It is one of the most beautiful roads in the world, a delightful drive in any season. Travelling it, you will head roughly north from a junction 2.7 kilometres west of Lake Louise to Jasper some 230 kilometres away. The road is currently cleared in winter and, avoiding times when blizzards blow through the high passes, is especially spectacular at that time of year — when the falls freeze into ice, the snow is piled high beside the road, and caribou visit the valleys. One of the delights of this well-maintained, two-lane highway is the fact that the old one-lane road is still visible in many places nearby, a subtle reminder of the former means of access.

Legendary outfitter/guide Jimmy Simpson, who built the first Num-Ti-Jah Lodge[62] at Bow Lake in the 1920s, was instrumental in building the original road from Lake Louise to Jasper. Construction began in 1931, with Simpson blazing the trail that would become the route to Bow Lake, for a fee of $75:

"They gave me the contract and I came up and did it all in one day. I came up in the evening and got as far as Hector Lake, camped under a tree at night, finished it the next day and went back to Lake Louise and caught the train to Banff."[63]

The road was completed as far as Bow Pass in 1935, with the soft muskeg along Bow Lake causing constant delays. By 1939, the delays were overcome, and the road officially opened in 1940, allowing motoring visitors to travel between Banff and Lake Louise and Jasper, and conveniently stay at Num-Ti-Jah Lodge overnight. The close proximity of glaciers to the road and the comforts of the lodge drew artists to paint at Bow Lake and in the nearby valleys and passes.

Crowfoot Glacier was named at the turn of the century for its three-toed appearance, but has receded so much that it now looks as if the crow is minus one toe. Historical artworks are often a telling record of the changes in mountain features, including the effects of fire, avalanches, glacial advance and recession, and varying water levels. Catharine Whyte, together with her husband Peter, made several trips into the Bow Lake area to paint, stopping along the way to capture the toes of Crowfoot Glacier.

They stayed with the Simpsons at Bow Lake, and usually walked out to painting destinations in the surrounding areas. On August 8, 1941, they arrived for a few days of sketching. Their careful observations on the conditions of each day's weather and on the scenery, indicate the shortness of the summer season

at high altitude locations:

" It does feel good to be up here and painting again. We are in a little cabin and it works very well. Hardly anyone wanders over this way and yet if we want to be sociable the chalet is near… We started painting this morning, but the sky has turned milky… The flies are buzzing which often means rain, so I hope the weather won't turn bad now that we have gotten up here… The flowers have all gone. I think the snow storm last week must have finished them. It must have been lovely up here when they were all out for the remains are thick."[64]

Catharine Robb Whyte
Crowfoot Glacier, 1945-55
oil on canvas, Whyte Museum of the Canadian Rockies

THE MAIN ATTRACTION
AUTUMN'S GOLDEN LARCHES

As word of the spectacular painting grounds of the Rocky Mountains spread among artists, the time to go for the best scenery was always fall, a time that is known as "the height of the larches."

In mid-September and early October, the larches work their magic. Larches, more specifically, the Lyall's larch, found in the eastern Rockies in the upper subalpine forest at tree line, are deciduous conifers. Each fall, their needles act like leaves, turn colour, and drop.

Several characteristics combine to produce the magnificent autumn display so admired by hikers, photographers and artists. First, larches are often found in pure stands on rocky terrain with little other tree growth to hide them. Second, they usually turn colour "en masse" creating a vast expanse of vivid gold. Third, their trunks and branches are black and knobby, contrasting dramatically both in colour with the saffron gold of the needles, and in texture with the spiky appearance of the needles. And finally, they have an overall raggedy silhouette, stunted and misshapen, which gives a sort of trollish charm to their stunning gold colour.

Larches have personality. They are old men in rich robes, beggars in brocade. Often they sprinkle their needles onto patches of new autumn snow, like fresh orange peel on a white-iced cupcake. There are few more delightful fall sensations than walking through a stand of recently seared larches, with cold air in your lungs and the sweet smell of autumn ripeness in the air.

The fall attraction of larches, however, should not be considered their only performance. In spring, the stubby branches are covered with a black, downy fuzz, and sprout feather-soft, apple-green needles from each warty bump. Running your hand over a branch is always a pleasant surprise, no prickles!

1. Hansa Yellow Light
2. Light Cadmium Yellow
3. Cadmium Yellow, Medium
4. Cadmium Yellow
5. Cadmium Orange
6. Yellow Ochre
7. Mars Yellow
8. Cadmium Red
9. Raw Sienna
10. Burnt Sienna
11. Burnt Umber
12. Brown Madder
13. Van Dyke Brown

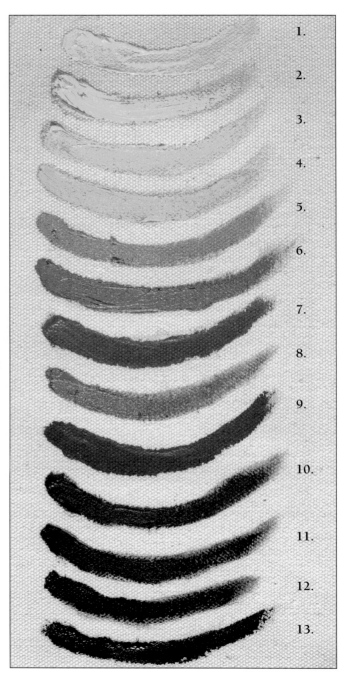

Catharine Robb Whyte
Mount Temple, Larches, 1940
oil on canvas, Whyte Museum of the Canadian Rockies

Frederick Brigden
Bow Lake, undated, watercolour on paper
Glenbow Collection

"NEVER HAVE I SEEN A LAKE LOOK MORE BEAUTIFUL
THAN ON THAT FAIR MORNING IN JUNE. IT WAS AS
BLUE AS THE SKY COULD MAKE IT, THE ICE REFLECTED
THE MOST VIVID GREEN; IN THE DISTANCE A FINE
GLACIER SWEPT TO THE LAKESHORE, WHOSE EVERY
CREVASSE WAS A BRILLIANT BLUE LINE; THE BLEAK
GREY MOUNTAINS TOWERED ABOVE, AT OUR FEET
THE BRIGHT SPRING FLOWERS BLOOMED IN THE
GREEN GRASS, AND OVER ALL HUNG A DEEP BLUE
SKY. AROUND US HOVERED THE PEACE WHICH
ONLY THE BEAUTY AND SILENCE OF THE HILLS
COULD PORTRAY."

— Mary Schäffer at Bow Lake in *A Hunter of Peace*, 1907

BOW LAKE

The Bow Lake viewpoint, 34.5 kilometres from the beginning of the Icefields Parkway in the southeast, is worthy of a stop even though you can have a good look at Bow Lake as you travel past it in your car. The lake is all the more pleasant without the hum of an engine. When the road was built, several of Jimmy Simpson's regular out-fitting clients wrote to him, despairing of the develop-ment. Simpson, with mixed feelings, but likely banking on the success of Num-Ti-Jah to see him through the Depression, wrote back:

"I feel like you as regards the motor road up into the north country. When I recall the old days when I used to sleep out at night and under the stars and a spruce with 20 below as the only covering, it makes me feel that I don't want to see the same landmarks from an auto. I suppose the wind will blow with the same frigidity: the same ridges will be windswept and the same hollows will be drifted full even though the motor road passes over or by them, but to me the landscape will hold a blight or a scar that will never heal. Oh well, times must and will change. The youngsters of the present day accept the changed conditions as a matter of course just as we did in our
day and I suppose we ought to look ahead instead of backward. After all the trail in the making is more interesting than the one made previously, like the peak to be climbed for the first time instead of the last."[65]

Frederick Brigden was born in London and came to Canada as a child. He studied at the Central Ontario School of Art, at the Art Students League in New York, and with prominent Canadian artists William Cruikshank and George Reid. He worked at, and later became president of, the Toronto engraving firm Brigden's Limited, and was a founder member of many Canadian art associations. He lived most of his life in Toronto, but made numerous sketching trips throughout Canada, painting in water-colour the scenery from Cape Breton to the Rockies. He was closely associated with the Group of Seven as it began to take shape, and subscribed to the creed that artists should look to Canadian subjects for inspiration. His soft, even-toned depiction of Bow Lake looks south from the meadows at the head of the lake, back towards Crowfoot Mountain.

Charles Comfort
Mount Athabasca, undated
oil on board
Collection of Don and Shirley Grace

"THE FIRST IMPACT OF THE [GROUP OF SEVEN]…
ON ME AS A YOUNG STUDENT WAS ONE OF
BURGEONING COLOUR. THE SECOND WAS THE
DYNAMIC, ALMOST RUTHLESS ENERGY EMPLOYED
IN THE USE OF PAINT. THE THIRD WAS THE…
SUBJECT MATTER… THE OVERWHELMING THEME
WAS THE VIGOROUS BEAUTIFUL CHALLENGE OF
THE LITTLE-KNOWN WILDERNESS OF THE NORTH,
THE UNCONQUERED TERRITORY OF UNEXPLORED
AND UNCLAIMED NATURAL TREASURE THAT WAS
SUDDENLY REVEALED…."

— Charles Comfort, upon first seeing an exhibition of
    work by the Group of Seven in 1920

MOUNT ATHABASCA

At kilometre 127 on the Icefields Parkway heading northwest, you will reach the Columbia Icefield. This vast, frozen icefield covers a total area of 325 square kilometres, most of which is high above the road, hidden from view. Mount Athabasca, however, can be clearly seen.

Charles Comfort was born in Scotland in 1900, and immigrated to Winnipeg in 1912, where he began a long and esteemed career in the arts. He studied with Alexander Musgrove at the Winnipeg School of Art from 1916 to 1919 and at the Art Students League of New York in the early 20s. He taught at the Ontario College of Art, the University of Toronto, and the Banff School of Fine Arts. He became director of the National Gallery of Canada in 1960, and was an official Canadian war artist from 1943 to 1946.

Comfort's depiction of the uppermost portion of Mount Athabasca captures the glacier in scratchy, chalky white. It is a simple, clean work, uncomplicated in design. The brushwork, which runs in sweeping, harsh strokes all over the surface of the work, conveys the patterns of glacial ice as they scar the surface of the Athabasca Glacier.

TRAIL INFO

Trail information: The Icefields Parkway
Type of hike: Roadside view
Best time to go: In clear weather, year-round
Distance: 230 km
Elevation gain: The highest point on the Parkway is Bow Summit, at 2069 m
Driving time: Allow 4 hrs if you wish to stop and enjoy the numerous viewpoints
Route: The junction of the Icefields Parkway and the Trans-Canada Highway is 2.7 km west of Lake Louise. The site of Brigden's water-colour is at 34.5 km; you can park at the Bow Lake viewpoint, just south of the access road to Num-Ti-Jah Lodge. Non-guests are discouraged from parking in the lodge parking lot. Continue on the Parkway, heading northwest past Peyto Lake, Waterfowl Lake, and Saskatchewan River Crossing. There are many viewpoints if you wish to stop. After climbing the Big Bend hill, (an elevation gain of 425 m), at kilometre 133, stop at the Sunwapta Canyon viewpoint. This is an excellent spot from which to view the site of Charles Comfort's composition depicting Athabasca Glacier.

"LIKE FEUDAL LORDS (AND LADIES) WE SAT AT OUR MIDDAY MEAL OF TINNED-MEAT AND BANNOCK THAT DAY. OUR TABLE, THE CLEAN SWEET EARTH ITSELF, WAS GARNISHED WITH FLOWERS, WITH VETCHES CRIMSON, YELLOW, AND PINK. THEY SPREAD AWAY IN EVERY DIRECTION FROM US AS FAR AS THE EYE COULD SEE, AND, THE WARM WINDS BLOWING DOWN UPON US FROM THE SOUTHERN VALLEYS, SWEPT ACROSS THEIR FACES AND BORE THEIR CLOVER-LADEN BREATH TO THE FIRST WHITE GUESTS OF THAT WONDERFUL REGION."

— Mary T.S. Schäffer, upon her discovery of Maligne Lake, 1908

Lawren Harris
Maligne Lake, c.1940
tempera on board
McMichael Canadian Art Collection

MALIGNE LAKE

MALIGNE LAKE

If you drive west from the city of Calgary, through the foothills and Kananaskis Country, past Lake Louise, and up the panoramic Icefields Parkway, you will cross the boundary between Banff National Park and Jasper National Park in about 3.5 hours. Another hour will take you into Jasper townsite, and another 45 minutes up a winding, hilly road will deliver you to the magnificent "cubist's paradise"[66] of the Maligne Valley. The Tonquin Valley lies to the southwest, where the impenetrable Ramparts border Mount Robson Provincial Park.

In the early 1900s, Maligne Lake was known to the Stoney Indians as Chaba Imne (Beaver Lake), and reported to lie somewhere in the area around Mount Brazeau, which was largely unmapped. American botanist Mary Schäffer met Sir James Hector, geologist of the Palliser expedition, at Glacier House in 1903. His tales of his adventures, the thrill of the unknown, and the joys of exploration, stimulated her desire to explore unknown regions of the Rockies. Exploration was largely the domain of what Schäffer referred to as "the masculine element" in the early 1900s, but she determined that the feminine element could "starve as well as they; the muskeg will be no softer for us than them; the ground no harder to sleep upon; the waters no deeper to swim, nor the bath colder if we fall in."[67] She made an unsuccessful attempt to find Maligne Lake in 1907, and to assist her search, Stoney Indian Sampson Beaver drew a map to the lake from memory of a trip there when he was 14 years old. It was "Stowed away in the pocket of the...travel worn diary...and in the pocket of our minds the determination to find it."[68]

The following year, with the help of Beaver's accurate map, a second attempt was made. Despite hordes of mosquitoes, spongy soft valleys, and many misleading little rivers that looked as if they could not possibly come from a lake of any great size, Schäffer's party finally:

"...stood upon its shores, we looked across to the other side, wondered what it all held in store for us...The unknown has a glamour indescribable; it creeps into the blood; it calls silently, but nonetheless its call is irresistible and strong.

Yes, the long quest was over, the object found, and it seemed very beautiful to our partial eyes."[69]

The group named a number of the surrounding peaks that day. Mount Unwin after guide Sid Unwin, Mount Warren after guide Billy Warren, Samson Peak and Samson Narrows after Sampson Beaver, and in thanks to his accurate map, Leah Peak after Sampson's wife, and Mount Mary Vaux after the friend whose invitation to visit Glacier House in 1889 had first introduced Schäffer to the Rockies.

"JACKSON PITS HIS STATURE AGAINST THAT OF NATURE AND

ACCEPTS HIS FAILURES AND HIS SUCCESSES WITH HUMILITY. TO HIM A

RELATIONSHIP OF FORM, COLOUR AND SPACE ARE PROBLEMS

TO BE SOLVED ON THE SPOT, LIKE PADDLING A

CANOE IN A STIFF GALE, EACH DIP OF THE BLADE A NEW PROBLEM…

A TOPOGRAPHICAL MAP OF CANADA WOULD BE DOTTED AS

WITH A RASH MARKING THE SPOTS WHERE HE HAS SCRAPED HIS PALETTE

KNIFE ON THE ROCKS OR CLEANED HIS BRUSHES ON A PINE LOG."

— Arthur Lismer in *A.Y. Jackson: Painter of Canada – An Appreciation*, undated

Lawren Harris
Mount Sampson, Maligne Lake, c.1924
oil on board, Private Collection

"HIS MOUNTAINS RISE LIKE GREAT TEETH OF

COSMIC LINE OUT OF CALM LAKE PEDESTALS AND

ARE AS SCULPTURAL, AS ENIGMATICALLY MATHEMATICAL

AS EPSTEIN. HE ACHIEVES A REMARKABLE STRUCTURAL

SYNTHESIS AND PRESENTS LANDSCAPE PURGED

OF ITS GROSSNESS OF DETAIL IN QUINTESSENTIAL

SYMBOLISM."

— *Toronto Mail and Empire*, on Lawren Harris, 1926

MOUNT SAMPSON, MALIGNE LAKE

When Lawren Harris and A.Y. Jackson came to Jasper in August of 1924, they went into the backcountry, not finding the views around the Jasper Park Lodge, where they were staying, to their liking. Together they bushwhacked a trail on the east shore of Maligne Lake, somewhere near the Samson Narrows, and up above the tree line. They returned that September and:

"Started early in the morning to tote our bedrolls, small tent, sketching material, and food for ten days up to this spot. The going was tough, and so it was not until late that same evening that we were settled. We pitched the tent just above the timber line on sloping ground, there being no level location. I built up a pile of crossed sticks under the foot of my bedroll so that it was level. Jackson did not bother to do the same; he simply crawled into his bedroll and went to sleep. Next morning at sunrise I awoke and glanced over to where Jackson was when I last saw him. I looked out of the tent flap and there he was twenty feet below, pulled up against a rock, buried in his bedroll, still fast asleep."[70]

Jackson and Harris spent a week at Maligne Lake in "a weird and ancient country of crumbling mountains and big glaciers"[71] before moving on to the Athabasca and Tonquin Valleys. They returned to the original Maligne camp for more sketching at the end of their trip. *Maligne Lake* depicts the view from about one kilometre down the lake from the main boat dock, out on the water. The rocks that Harris has placed at the bottom edge of the work anchor the scene. Look down the lake from the boat dock to get your bearings within the painting. Your view will match the work increasingly as you travel down the lake and the jutting, angular ridge of Samson Peak takes shape, and the mountains of the Queen Elizabeth Range and Mount Maligne march off down the horizon line on the left half of the work. Harris would later rework his studies into the canvas known as *Maligne Lake, Jasper Park* (not illustrated), in which he has stylized, conicalized, and smoothed the peaks into undulating, serene shapes, that border the still expanse of water. He said: "Real art never seeks factual truth. It seeks to express the character and spirit of a scene in its own plastic language...."[72]

Charles Comfort
Ramparts, Amethyst Lake, Tonquin Valley, Jasper, c.1949
oil on canvas
Collection of Don and Shirley Grace

"THE TONQUIN VALLEY HAS KEPT ITS BEAUTY

SECRET – AS IF IT HAD KNOWN WE WERE COMING,

IT WITHDREW SHYLY BEHIND VEILS OF MIST AND

FOR FIVE DAYS HAS MOCKED US WITH THE WIND,

THE RAIN, AND THE SNOW. "

— Charles Comfort entry in Amethyst Lakes Lodge guest
    book, August 27, 1948

THE TONQUIN VALLEY

RAMPARTS, AMETHYST LAKE, TONQUIN VALLEY, JASPER

The imposing face of the Gog quartzite formation known as The Ramparts was named for the fortress-like quality of its impenetrable face. Parapet, Dungeon, Redoubt, Turret, and Barbican are the individual peak names. These guard the waters of the Amethyst Lakes. The northern Ramparts, Bastion, and Drawbridge are circled by Moat Lake. They are an awe-inspiring sight, trapping clouds against their faces and soaring to heights of 900 metres above the waters of the lakes below.

Charles Fraser Comfort was a painter, muralist, printmaker, and illustrator. He began his career in the arts in Canada at the well-known commercial firm of Brigden's in Winnipeg, and later worked for their Toronto office for a time. He painted a number of public murals, including those at the National Library in Ottawa, the Hotel Vancouver (moved to the Art Gallery of Charlottetown in 1973), and the Toronto Stock Exchange. He served as Director of the National Gallery of Canada from 1960 to 1965, and retired from his duties there to concentrate on painting, continuing to accept mural commissions, and painting landscape and portraits.

It was at Brigden's in Toronto that Comfort met Will Ogilvie, an artist with whom he developed a deep friendship, shared a studio, and served as a Canadian war artist. They took several sketching trips together in Ontario and the Maritimes. In 1948 they went together to Jasper National Park, and were taken by pack horse to the Brewster outfitter's cabin on the shore of the Amethyst Lakes.

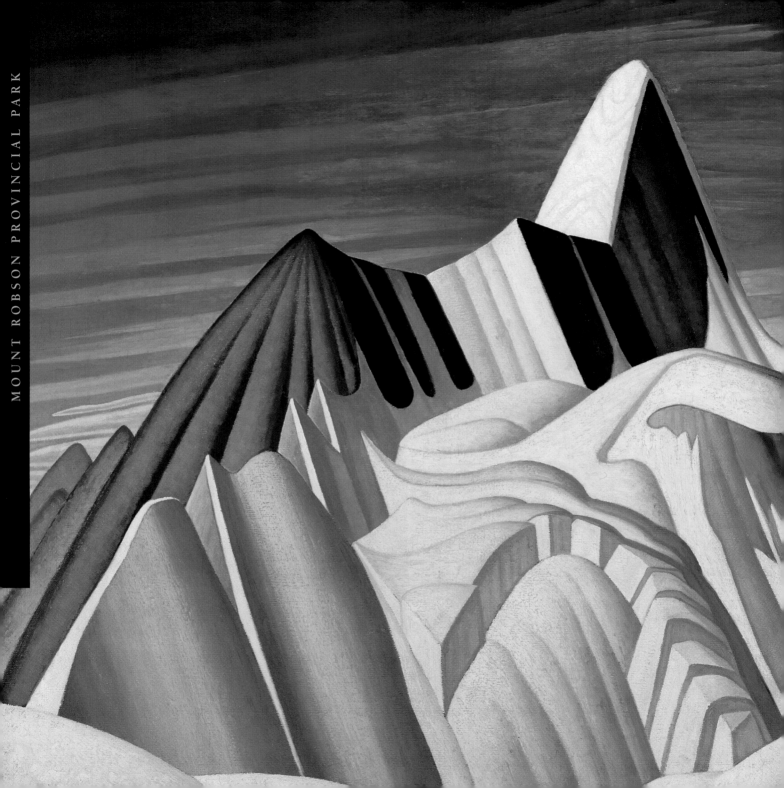

"TOWERING MAJESTICALLY ABOVE BERG LAKE,

THE TWO-KILOMETRE HIGH NORTH FLANK OF MOUNT

ROBSON EPITOMIZES THE GRANDEUR OF THE

CANADIAN ROCKIES. CLAD WITH A MAGNIFICENT

ARRAY OF GLACIERS, THIS MONOLITH OF ROCK,

SNOW, AND ICE IS WITHOUT EQUAL IN A

RANGE OF MOUNTAINS CELEBRATED FOR ITS

SPECTACULAR SCENERY."

— Graeme Pole in *Classic Hikes in the Canadian Rockies,* 1994

Lawren Harris
Mount Robson, c.1929
oil on canvas, McMichael Canadian Art Collection

A.Y. Jackson
Mount Robson, Resplendent and Kain, 1914
oil on panel, McMichael Canadian Art Collection

"YOU OUGHT TO SEE THOSE PROSPECTOR'S BOOTS
I BROUGHT OUT WITH ME, WORN ALL TO BITS. I'VE
BEEN CLIMBING EIGHT AND NINE THOUSAND FEET TO
SKETCH, AND USING THEM FOR A PILLOW AT NIGHT…
I HAVE A WHOLE RAFT OF SKETCHES, MANY OF THEM
UP TO THE STANDARD, BUT THIS COUNTRY IS LESS
PAINTABLE THAN NORTHERN ONTARIO."

— A.Y. Jackson to Dr. James McCallum, 1914

MOUNT ROBSON,
RESPLENDENT AND KAIN

The massive peak of Mount Robson, long thought to be the highest in the Canadian Rockies at 3954 metres, towers over the fertile and lush British Columbia forest below. It can be seen from many points along the steep 20 kilometre trail that leads to Berg Lake, or from the highway on the valley floor. In 1914, when A.Y. Jackson and J.W. Beatty came to the Robson area with hopes of a possible commission to paint the construction camps of the Canadian Northern Railway, this massive peak must have beckoned them.

This was Jackson's first trip to the West, and he was eager to explore the painting possibilities of the mountains. Jackson and Beatty painted along the rail line, depicting the camps and adjacent scenery, but Jackson found the work along the tracks rather dull, and "old" Beatty was not up to climbing to higher altitudes (at the time, J.W. Beatty was 44, Jackson 31). With an engineer along for safety, company, and as a guide, Jackson left the trackside and learned how to "get about in the mountains with neither blankets nor tent, on a diet restricted to bread, oatmeal, bacon, and tea."[73]

Jackson seems to have enjoyed the rigors of these hikes a great deal:

"We had good times in the mountains, and exciting ones. We took many chances, sliding down snow slopes with only a stick for a brake, climbing over glaciers without ropes, and crossing rivers too swift to wade, by felling trees across them."[74]

However the artistic pleasures did not exceed the physical ones. Very few works, aside from a few pencil drawings depicting the mountains at Yellowhead Pass in his sketchbook from 1914, are known from this trip. He recalls in his 1958 autobiography *A Painter's Country*:

"I made many sketches which were never used, as the railway which had commissioned them went bankrupt during the war. Later I came to the conclusion that the mountains were not my line, and I kept throwing sketches into the furnace until there was none left."[75]

Even as late as about 1968, Jackson was throwing his mountain drawings into the fire.[76] The "later" that he referred to here is an uncertain date, but likely refers to a time after his second trip to the Rockies, with Lawren Harris in 1924.

Jackson was not satisfied with his 1924 work any more than the work from 1914, admitting again that the mountains were not his subject. He seems to have been uncomfortable with his lacklustre results from the two trips, and in his writings for *Canadian Forum* criticizes the genre of mountain painting as a whole:

"Why is it that mountains which are so impressive in nature should be so unimpressive in a painting?… Few artists have enhanced their reputations by painting mountains and it would seem that the greater the mountain the more insignificant the artist who paints it becomes."[77]

Shortly after this, he recants:

"Copying mountains literally has been done to death. As inspiring motives for the creative artist they are a source of unlimited wealth of design, rhythm, form, and colour. The kodachrome boys can take care of the rest."[78] So much for A.Y. and the Rockies.

The sketch *Mount Robson, Resplendent and Kain*, is set looking towards the three peaks of Mount Robson, Resplendent Mountain, and Mount Kain, from a location southeast of the southern Kinney Lake campground and on the north flank of Campion Mountain. The work does not attempt to capture the majestic qualities of the famous peak, but instead depicts a quieter side, with rolling bands of thickly laid colour and Laurentianesque pattern.

"To show how bad the weather was, from

August 1 to September 10, that is to say forty-one

days, on twenty eight of these days it was

either snowing or raining all day or wet during

some part of the twenty-four hours. On three

separate occasions snow was lying thick at the

bottom of the valley."

– J.N. Collie in *The Alpine Journal,* 1910

MOUNT ROBSON

If you leaf through the many guide books and picture books that include photographs of Mount Robson, you will see a sharp outline of a white peak against clear blue sky, over and over again. Owen Staples's watercolour of Mount Robson, shrouded in wet, misty clouds, is more likely true to the average day at the peak. Mount Robson is so massive that it creates its own unique weather patterns, very different from the weather of the greater Jasper and Yellowhead areas. The forest surrounding Mount Robson is a British Columbia rainforest, full of unique plants and lush greenery. The valley elevation is low, and the rainforest-like climate is one of the mildest (and wettest) in the Rockies. A guide who travelled the Fraser River 29 times in 1862 recorded actually seeing the peak only once.

But Robson's weather can also change very rapidly, sometimes bringing the sun, more often bringing clouds, and making Robson a constant challenge for climbers. Due to poor weather, no parties are known to have made successful climbs between 1939 and 1953. It is fitting to include a cloud-capped scene for those that might make the two to three day trek into the region and find the peaks obscured.

Owen Staples was born in Somerset, England, in 1866 and immigrated to Hamilton as a child. He later studied at the Rochester Art Club, New York, the Pennsylvania Academy of the Fine Arts, and at the Toronto Art Students League. Staples worked as an illustrator, a muralist, and a cartoonist, in addition to painting landscape in watercolour. He was a member of the Ontario Society of Artists, and later served as president of the Arts and Letters Club in Toronto. Information surrounding his sketching activity in the West is scant, but was likely conducted in preparation for his work illustrating *The Backwoods of Canada,* by C.P. Traill, which was published in 1929.

Owen Staples
Mount Robson, 1922
watercolour on paper, Glenbow Collection

Lawren Harris
Tumbling Glacier, Berg Lake, c.1929
oil on panel, Private Collection

"'LANDSCAPE' IS A CONCEPT THAT POINTS IN
TWO DIRECTIONS, TO THE PICTURE IN THE FRAME
AND TO THE PART OF THE WORLD OUTSIDE THE
FRAME, AND THEREFORE RAISES UNAVOIDABLE
QUESTIONS ABOUT THE RELATION BETWEEN ART
AND REALITY... IT SEEMS TO ME REASONABLE
TO SUPPOSE THAT EACH ARTIST...FIRST STOOD IN
FRONT OF A LANDSCAPE AND FELT...AWED BY
SOMETHING VASTLY GREATER THAN HIS OR HER
KNOWLEDGE."

— Jeremy Hooker in *The Experience of Landscape*, 1987

TUMBLING GLACIER, BERG LAKE

The glacier above Berg Lake was originally named Blue Glacier by A.P. Coleman in about 1908. The name was then changed to Tumbling Glacier, and applied to this work by Lawren Harris in about 1929. The name of the glacier has since been changed to Berg Glacier, as the Tumbling Glacier name was already in use in Wolverine Pass in the Kootenays. The composition looks directly across Berg Lake towards Mount Robson, from a point about halfway up the northwest shore of the lake along the main trail. There are many places to stop and enjoy the setting of Harris's scene on this part of the trail, where intermittent benches can be found. The view you will see is much the same and varies only slightly when the small icebergs break off the glacier and float across the water, pushed by a tailwind towards you.

TRAIL INFO

Trail information:
Mount Robson
Type of hike: Overnight backpack
Best time to go: Summer
Trailhead: The Berg Lake parking lot is at the end of a 2 km side road which begins at the Mount Robson Information Centre parking lot on the Yellowhead Highway between Valemont and Jasper.
Distance: 19.6 km to Berg Lake campground
Elevation gain: 784 m
Degree of difficulty: Difficult, due to the length of the trail and several steep sections
Hiking time: Allow 2-3 days
Topo map: 83 E/3
Route: The trail begins at the Berg Lake parking lot and roughly follows the Robson River for 4.2 km to Kinney Lake. There is a viewpoint at 5.2 km, and campgrounds at Kinney Lake at 6.7 km and Whitehorn Mountain at 10.5 km. The trail is clearly marked and obvious all the way, and is the most heavily travelled backpacking trail in the Canadian Rockies. The climb begins at the top of Kinney Lake as it runs through the Valley of a Thousand Falls, a steep valley into which many, if not thousands, of ribbons of water cascade. The steepest switchbacks begin after you have crossed the suspension bridge past the Whitehorn campground. The tough climb is broken by incredible views of Emperor Falls. There is a viewpoint for these falls at 14.3 km and a campground at 15 km. Continue on past the campground (most of the climbing is over now) and watch as the views of Mount Robson become increasingly spectacular. There are several more campgrounds in the vicinity of Berg Lake, which you will reach at 19.6 km.

The preparation of this book has been a time of wonder and discovery. It began with Lawren Harris, and one of life's coincidences – my having hiked to Tumbling Glacier the week before I first saw his oil sketch of the same name. As I viewed the painting, the frame no longer defined its edges. Instead, they faded into the sounds and smells of the woods, escapades with porcupines, and the warmth of tea brewed in an enamel cup. From the first inkling of an idea, to reading through travel journals in archives across the country, preparing for each backpacking trip, and seeing the project become a book, this sense of discovery prevails. I have abandoned my suits for hiking boots and an anorak.

I have a clear and vivid memory of lying in the forest undergrowth on the shore of Maligne Lake near Spirit Island, in Jasper National Park, while reading Lawren Harris's account of his trip to the same place with A.Y. Jackson. I had read that account many times before, but while lying on that same earth, with the smell of trout lifting off the water, and swallows buzzing after the same flies that called those trout, his stories were all the more humorous, all the more interesting and pertinent, because of where I was.

If you were to hike around the Canadian Rockies with your eyes to the ground, looking for the post holes of every artist's easel or sketching seat that had been planted there, you would find dents in every lakeshore, at the foot of every glacier, and at the base of every waterfall from the 49th parallel north. Next to these dents, the dried remains of paint scrapings still cling to branches and blend with the patterns of lichen on rocks. Broken-off brushes and blobs of discarded paint, are tiny hints and reminders of the activity of painting in the mountains, easily overlooked.

The more tangible evidence of the artists' presence in the Rockies cannot be overlooked. In pen and ink, watercolour, oil, print media, pencil, and pastel, the varied topography of the Rocky Mountains has been recorded by generations of artists. There are more works, depicting the ends of more trails that my boots have yet to take me to. Watercolours of waterfalls, woodblock prints of larches and mountains, and oils of glacial snow and ice, are found in public and private collections from coast to coast. They hang on the white walls of galleries and in homes and offices, carefully tended and admired. We conserve them, exhibit and write about them, contemplate them, and guard them carefully. They are venerated, iconized, and a source of great national pride. Yet they are far removed from the places that inspired them.

The purpose of this book is to reconnect these works with the places that were their inspiration, to take the art off the gallery wall and out to the wilderness places in which it was created. It is an effort to foster another way of looking at art, and another way of enjoying the Canadian Rocky Mountains. It is my hope that the conclusion of this book will not mark the end of the trail for the hiker and the reader, but instead the start of a fulfilling pastime, the beginning of a delightful journey of discovery, wonder, and surprise.

"THERE IS IN THE SOUL OF MAN A PASSIONATE UNSATISFIED LONGING FOR BEAUTY.

AS THE COMPLEX NATURE OF MAN-MADE EXISTENCE OF THE MODERN WORLD TURNS ITS

MACHINERY AND ITS KNOWLEDGE OF SCIENCE TOWARDS THE COMFORT OF HUMANITY,

IT YET AGGRAVATES THE DISCONTENT WHICH IS EVIDENT AROUND US. OUR

POLLUTED CITIES, OUR MECHANICAL FASHION OF LIVING, OUR UGLY SQUALID ARCHITECTURE,

OUR COMMERCIAL PRIDE AND FOOLISHNESS, AND CHEAP ENTICING ENTERTAINMENT,

ARE ALL SQUEEZING THE BEAUTY OUT OF LIFE, AND MAKING US A STANDARDIZED

DISDAINFUL PEOPLE. WE CUT AND SLASH OUR TREES TO MAKE ROOM FOR UGLY BUILDINGS;

WE FILL IN AND STAMP OUT THE NATURAL BEAUTY OF OUR CITIES;

WE CARRY INTO THE VAST HINTERLAND OUR CITY BANALITIES, AND PREY UPON ITS DENIZENS…

THE STILL SMALL VOICE OF ART-CONSCIOUSNESS, WHICH IS THE SILENT PROTEST

AGAINST UGLINESS IN ENVIRONMENT, IS NEARLY HUSHED. WE TRY TO RECREATE IT BY

FILLING ART GALLERIES AND MUSEUMS WITH THE DRY BONES OF THE PAST…

BUT LET US NOT MISTAKE THIS FOR ART. ART LIES NOT IN POSSESSION NOR IN PRIDE

OF OWNERSHIP… ART IS A CREATIVE LIVING FORCE. IF WE SHOULD HAVE BEAUTY

AGAIN IN OUR LIVES, WE SHALL HAVE TO LISTEN… TO THE IMPRESS OF SIGHTS AND

SOUNDS OF BEAUTY… THE DEVELOPMENT OF THE ARTIST IN EACH OF US IS THE

RESPONSE TO THESE VITAL SPIRITUAL RHYTHMS OF EXISTENCE."

— Arthur Lismer in *Art and Life,* 1927

**Frederic Marlett (F.M.) Bell-Smith
(1846 – 1923)**
Morning, Lake Louise, 1909
watercolour on board
44.5 x 59.4
59.34.7
Glenbow Collection, purchased, 1959

**Frederick Henry Brigden
(1871 – 1956)**
Bow Lake, undated
watercolour on paper
24.6 x 34.7
990.53.2
Glenbow Collection, purchased with
funds from the Glenbow Museum
Acquisitions Society, 1990

**Belmore Browne
(1880 – 1954)**
*After September Snow (Lake Louise,
Canadian Rockies)*, undated
oil on canvas
50.8 x 60.6
58.34.1
Glenbow Collection, purchased, 1958

Rainy Day at Marvel Lake, 1934
oil on canvas
30.5 x 40.6
55.48.15
Glenbow Collection, gift of
Mrs. Belmore Browne, 1955

Rising Clouds, Lake Louise, undated
oil on canvas
40.6 x 50.8
58.34.12
Glenbow Collection, purchased, 1958

Spring Reflections (Mount Rundle),
undated
oil on canvas
45.7 x 60.9
58.34.14
Glenbow Collection, purchased, 1958

**Charles Fraser Comfort
(1900 – 1994)**
Mount Athabasca, undated
oil on board
24.0 x 29.3
Collection of Don and Shirley Grace

*Ramparts, Amethyst Lake, Tonquin Valley,
Jasper*, c.1949
oil on canvas
59.0 x 75.0
Collection of Don and Shirley Grace

Kathleen (Kay) Daly (1898 – 1994)
Moraine Lake, undated
oil on canvas board
40.4 x 50.8
990.49.3
Glenbow Collection, purchased with
funds from the Glenbow Museum
Acquisitions Society, 1987

**Thomas William Fripp
(1864 – 1931)**
*Lake in the Clouds, Lake Agnes,
Canadian Rockies*, 1922
watercolour on paper
44.0 x 32.5
Collection of Don and Shirley Grace

Mount Fairview from Mount Temple,
1918
watercolour on paper
27.3 x 37.5
62.115
Glenbow Collection, purchased, 1962

John Hammond (1843 – 1939)
The Three Sisters, after 1890
oil on canvas
137.2 x 198.1
60.79.3
Glenbow Collection, purchased, 1960

Lawren Stewart Harris (1885 – 1970)
Emerald Lake, c.1924
oil on panel
30.4 x 37.9
1969.7.2
McMichael Canadian Art Collection, in
Memory of T. Campbell Newman, Q.C.

Glaciers, Rocky Mountains, 1930
oil on card
30.5 x 38.1
45.A.49
Collection of the London Regional Art
and Historical Museums, F.B. Housser
Memorial Collection, 1945

Isolation Peak, Rocky Mountains, 1930
oil on canvas
106.7 x 127.0
HHPC46.1
Hart House Permanent Collection

Maligne Lake, c.1940
tempera on board
71.0 x 100.0
1968.19.1RV
McMichael Canadian Art Collection,
gift of Mr. C.A.G. Matthews

Mount Lefroy, 1930
oil on canvas
133.5 x 153.5
1975.7
McMichael Canadian Art Collection,
purchased, 1975

Mount Robson, c.1929
oil on canvas
128.3 x 152.4
1979.20
McMichael Canadian Art Collection,
purchased, 1979

Mount Sampson, Maligne Lake,
c.1924
oil on board
26.3 x 35.0
Private Collection

Mount Temple, undated
oil on heavyweight laminate
board
30.0 x 37.5
1968.25.11
McMichael Canadian Art
Collection, gift of Mr. C.A.G.
Matthews

Tumbling Glacier, Berg Lake, c.1929
oil on panel
30.2 x 37.1
Private Collection

**Lars Jonson Haukaness
(1862 – 1929)**
*Ptarmigan Pass, Canadian
Rockies*, 1928
oil on canvas
60.9 X 71.1
Collection of Don and Shirley Grace

**Alexander Young (A.Y.) Jackson
(1882 – 1974)**
Mount Robson, Resplendent and Kain,
1914
oil on panel
21.4 x 26.8
1968.8.23
McMichael Canadian Art Collection,
gift of Mrs. S. Walter Stewart

**Illingworth (Buck) Holey Kerr
(1905 – 1989)**
Ice and Still Water, Canmore, 1969
oil on canvas
55.9 x 76.2
72.2.4
Glenbow Collection, purchased, 1972

**Alfred Crocker (A.C.) Leighton
(1901 – 1965)**
Boulder Pass, Skoki, 1935
watercolour on paper
36.0 x 45.5
Private Collection

Floe Lake, Marble Canyon, 1930
watercolour on paper
37.1 x 47.0
70.43
Glenbow Collection, purchased, 1970

Mount Skoki, 1935
oil on canvas
76.2 x 101.6
Collection of the Leighton
Foundation

Mount Assiniboine, undated
oil on linen
66.3 x 76.6
89.19
Collection of The Edmonton Art
Gallery

**Barbara Mary (Barleigh) Leighton
(1911 – 1986)**
Mount Assiniboine, undated
colour woodcut on paper
36.0 x 44.0
63.80.2
Glenbow Collection, purchased, 1963

Mount Eisenhower, undated
colour woodcut on paper
32.5 x 41.2
63.80.3
Glenbow Collection, purchased, 1963

Arthur Lismer (1885 – 1969)
Cathedral Mountain, 1928
oil on canvas
121.9 x 142.2
1959.1219
Montreal Museum of Fine Arts,
gift of the A. Sidney Dawes Fund

The Glacier, 1928
oil on canvas
101.5 x 126.7
60.77.J
Art Gallery of Hamilton, gift of
the Women's Committee, 1960

**James Edward Hervey (J.E.H.)
MacDonald (1873 – 1932)**
Cathedral Peak and Lake O'Hara,
1927
oil on panel
21.4 x 26.6
1966.15.9
McMichael Canadian Art Collection,
gift of Mr. R.A. Laidlaw

*Clearing Weather, Sherbrooke Lake,
Above Wapta Lake*,
c.1928 or 1929
oil on cardboard
21.4 x 26.7
15500
National Gallery of Canada, Vincent
Massey Bequest, 1968

Lake McArthur, Yoho Park, 1924
oil on cardboard
21.4 x 26.6
15498
National Gallery of Canada, Vincent
Massey Bequest, 1968

Lake O'Hara with Snow, undated
oil on panel
21.3 x 26.5
79.6.1
Glenbow Collection, gift of
Mr. and Mrs. Max Stern, 1979

Wiwaxy Peaks, Lake O'Hara, 1926
oil on medium weight card
21.4 x 26.5
1968.25.15
McMichael Canadian Art Collection,
gift of Mr. C.A.G. Matthews

**James Williamson Galloway (Jock)
Macdonald (1897 – 1960)**
Lake McArthur, 1941
oil on board
36.8 x 28.8
Collection of Don and Shirley Grace

Mount Lefroy, Lake O'Hara, 1944
oil on canvas
81.3 x 101.6
1978.4.1
The University of British Columbia,
Morris and Helen Belkin Art Gallery

**Walter Joseph Phillips
(1884 – 1963)**
Mountain Road, 1942
colour woodcut on paper
22.8 x 33.1
55.26.67
Glenbow Collection, purchased, 1955

Mount Rundle, Banff, 1945
watercolour on paper
42.9 x 38.7
56.9.7
Glenbow Collection, purchased,
1956

**Carl Clemens Moritz Rungius
(1869 – 1959)**
Brachiopod Mountain, undated
oil on canvas
22.8 x 28.0
59.7.1390
Glenbow Collection, purchased,
1959

Crowfoot Glacier, undated
oil on canvas
19.0 x 27.9
59.7.1417
Glenbow Collection, purchased,
1959

Mountain Lake (Lake O'Hara), undated
oil on canvas
40.6 x 50.8
59.7.6
Glenbow Collection, purchased,
1959

Ptarmigan Peak, undated
oil on canvas
22.8 x 28.0
59.67.20
Glenbow Collection, purchased, 1960

Sage Brush (detail only – front cover),
undated
oil on canvas
23.0 x 28.0
59.7.1127
Glenbow Collection, purchased,
1959

John Singer Sargent (1856 – 1925)
Lake O'Hara, September, 1916, 1916
oil on canvas
122.5 x 141.5
1916.496
Fogg Art Collection, Harvard University
Art Museums, Louise E. Bettens Fund

Owen Staples (1866 – 1949)
Mount Robson, 1922
watercolour on paper
33.2 x 24.9
991.19.1
Glenbow Collection, purchased with
funds from the Glenbow Museum
Acquisitions Society, 1991

Catharine Robb Whyte (1906 – 1979)
Crowfoot Glacier, 1944-55
oil on canvas
27.7 x 35.2
WyC.01.143
Collection of the Whyte Museum of the
Canadian Rockies, gift of the Catharine
Robb Whyte Estate

In the High Country, Wiwaxy Peak, 1937
oil on canvas board
27.5 x 35.5
WyC.01.123
Collection of the Whyte Museum of the
Canadian Rockies, gift of the Catharine
Robb Whyte Estate

Mount Temple, Larches, 1940
oil on canvas
27.7 x 35.2
WyC.01.412
Collection of the Whyte Museum of the
Canadian Rockies, gift of the Catharine
Robb Whyte Estate

*On the Rock Pile, Looking West
(Wenkchemna)*, undated
oil on canvas
25.0 x 30.0
WyC.01.116
Collection of the Whyte Museum of the
Canadian Rockies, gift of the Catharine
Robb Whyte Estate

Peter Whyte (1905 – 1966)
From Larch Valley, Moraine Lake, undated
oil on canvas
28.0 x 35.4
WyP.01.184
Collection of the Whyte Museum of the
Canadian Rockies, gift of the Catharine
Robb Whyte Estate

Mount Assiniboine, September Snow,
c.1941
oil on canvas
64.0 x 76.0
WyP.02.09
Collection of the Whyte Museum of the
Canadian Rockies, gift of the Catharine
Robb Whyte Estate

BOOKS:

Adamson, Jeremy.
Lawren S. Harris: Urban Scenes and Wilderness Landscapes; 1906 – 1930. Toronto: Art Gallery of Ontario, 1978.

Anderson, Frank W., Harry Rowed, and Dave Stewart.
Majestic Jasper. Surrey: Frontier Books, 1980.

Beers, Don.
Banff – Assiniboine: A Beautiful World. Calgary: Highline Publishing, 1993.

——. *Jasper – Robson: A Taste of Heaven.* Calgary: Highline Publishing, 1996.

——. *The Wonder of Yoho.* Calgary: Rocky Mountain Books, 1989.

——. *The World of Lake Louise.* Calgary: Highline Publishing, 1991.

Boulet, Roger.
Frederic Marlett Bell-Smith, 1846 – 1923. Victoria: Art Gallery of Greater Victoria, 1977.

——. *The Tranquility and the Turbulence: The Life and Works of Walter J. Phillips.* Ontario: M.B. Loates Publishing, 1981.

Darroch, Lois.
Bright Land: A Warm Look at Arthur Lismer. Vancouver: Merritt Publishing Company, 1981.

Dutka, JoAnna, and Edward Cavell.
Kathleen Daly: Canmore Workings. Banff: Whyte Museum of the Canadian Rockies, 1987.

Duval, Paul.
Canadian Art, Vital Decades. Vancouver: Clarke, Irwin and Company Limited, 1970.

——. *The Tangled Garden.* Scarborough: Cerebus/Prentice-Hall, 1978.

Duval, Paul, et al.
A Heritage of Canadian Art. Toronto: Sampson Matthews Limited, 1976.

Fenton, Terry.
A.C. Leighton and the Canadian Rockies. Banff: Whyte Museum of the Canadian Rockies, 1989.

Fetherling, Douglas, ed.
Documents in Canadian Art. Peterborough: Broadview Press, 1987.

Fraser, Esther.
The Canadian Rockies: Early Travels and Explorations. Edmonton: Hurtig Publishers Limited, 1969.

——. *Wheeler.* Banff: Summerthought Limited, 1978.

Forster, Merna.
Jasper... A Walk in the Past. Jasper: Parks and People, 1987.

Gadd, Ben.
Handbook of the Canadian Rockies. Jasper: Corax Press, 1995.

Gray, Margaret Blair.
Charles Comfort. Agincourt: Gage Publishing, 1976.

Groves, Naomi Jackson.
A.Y.'s Canada. Vancouver: Clarke, Irwin and Company Limited, 1968.

Harper, J. Russell.
Paul Kane 1810 – 1871. Ottawa: The National Gallery of Canada, 1971.

——. *Painting in Canada: A History.* Toronto: University of Toronto Press, 1977.

Harper, J. Russell, et al.
Lawren Harris: Retrospective Exhibition, 1963. Vancouver: Seymour Press, 1963.

Harris, Bess, and R.G.P. Colgrove, eds.
Lawren Harris. Toronto: Macmillan of Canada, 1969.

Harris, Lawren S.
The Story of the Group of Seven. Toronto: Rous and Mann Press Limited, 1964.

Hart, E.J.
A Hunter of Peace. Banff: Whyte Museum of the Canadian Rockies, 1980.

——. *Jimmy Simpson, Legend of the Rockies.* Canmore: Altitude Publishing Canada Ltd., 1991.

Hart, E.J., and Jon Whyte.
Carl Rungius: Painter of the Western Wilderness. Calgary: Glenbow Museum; Vancouver: Douglas and MacIntyre, 1985.

Hill, Charles C.
The Group of Seven: Art for a Nation. Ottawa: The National Gallery of Canada; Ottawa: McClelland and Stewart, 1995.

Hooker, Jeremy.
The Experience of Landscape. London: South Bank Art Centre, 1987.

Hunter, E.R.
J.E.H. MacDonald: A Biography and Catalogue of his Work. Toronto: The Ryerson Press, 1940.

Jackson, A.Y.
A Painter's Country: The Autobiography of A.Y. Jackson. Toronto: Clarke, Irwin and Company Limited, 1958.

——. *Banting as an Artist.* Toronto: The Ryerson Press, 1943.

Jackson, Christopher.
North by West: The Arctic and Rocky Mountain Paintings of Lawren Harris, 1924 – 1931. Calgary: Glenbow Museum, 1991.

——. *With Lens and Brush: Images of the Western Canadian Landscape, 1845 – 1890.* Calgary: Glenbow Museum, 1989.

Kerr, Illingworth.
Paint and Circumstance. Calgary: Jules and Maureen Poscente, Ralph Hedlin, Heidi Redekop and Wm. H. Hopper, 1987.

Langshaw, Rick.
Geology of the Canadian Rockies. Banff: Summerthought Limited, 1989.

Larisey, Peter.
Light for a Cold Land: Lawren Harris's Work and Life – An Interpretation. Toronto: Dundurn Press, 1993.

McLeish, John A.B.
September Gale: A Study of Arthur Lismer of the Group of Seven. Toronto: J.M. Dent and Sons, 1955.

Mount, Charles Merrill.
John Singer Sargent, A Biography. New York: W.W. Norton and Company, Inc., 1969.

Murray, Joan.
The Best of the Group of Seven. Oshawa: The Robert McLaughlin Gallery, 1993.

Niven, Frederick.
Colour in the Canadian Rockies. Toronto: Thomas Nelson and Sons Limited, 1937.

Olson, Stanley
John Singer Sargent: His Portrait. New York: St. Martin's Press, 1986.

Patton, Brian.
Parkways of the Canadian Rockies. Banff: Summerthought Limited, 1982.

Patton, Brian, ed.
Tales from the Canadian Rockies. Edmonton: Hurtig Publishers Limited, 1984.

Patton, Brian, and Bart Robinson.
The Canadian Rockies Trail Guide: A Hikers Manual to the National Parks. 6th ed. Canmore: Devil's Head Press, 1994.

Pole, Graeme.
Classic Hikes in the Canadian Rockies. Canmore: Altitude Publishing Canada Ltd., 1994.

Putnam, Joyce.
Seven Years with the Group of Seven. Kingston: Quarry Press, 1992.

Putnam, William L., Glen W. Boles, and Roger W. Laurilla.
Place Names of the Canadian Alps. Revelstoke: Footprint Publishing, 1990.

Ratcliff, Carter.
John Singer Sargent. New York: Abbeville Press, 1982.

Reid, Dennis.
Atma Buddhi Manas: The Later Work of Lawren S. Harris. Toronto: Art Gallery of Ontario, 1985.
—. *Our Own Country Canada.* Ottawa: National Gallery of Canada, 1979.
—. *The Group of Seven.* Ottawa: National Gallery of Canada, 1970.
Render, Lorne E.
The Mountains and the Sky. Calgary: Glenbow-Alberta Institute; Calgary: McClelland Stewart West, 1974.
Sandford, Robert.
The Columbia Icefield. Banff: Altitude Publishing Canada Ltd., 1993.
—. *Yoho: A History and Celebration of Yoho National Park.* Banff: Altitude Publishing Canada Ltd., 1993.
Sokoloff, Carol Ann.
Eternal Lake O'Hara. Banff: Ekstasis Editions, 1992.
Thom, Ian.
Murals From a Great Train. Vancouver: Art Global, 1986.
Tippett, Maria, and Douglas Cole, eds.
Phillips in Print: The Selected Writings of Walter J. Phillips on Canadian Nature and Art. Winnipeg: The Manitoba Record Society, 1982.
Whiteman, Bruce.
J.E.H. MacDonald. Kingston: Quarry Press, 1995.
Whyte, Jon.
Mountain Glory: The Art of Peter and Catharine Whyte. Banff: Whyte Museum of the Canadian Rockies, 1988.
—. *Pete 'n' Catharine – Their Story.* Banff: Whyte Museum of the Canadian Rockies, 1989.
—. *Tommy and Lawrence: The Ways and the Trails of Lake O'Hara.* Banff: The Lake O'Hara Trails Club, 1983.

Wilkinson, Karen. *Painting in Alberta: An Historical Survey.* Edmonton: The Edmonton Art Gallery, 1980.
Zemans, Joyce.
Jock Macdonald. Ottawa: National Gallery of Canada, 1985.
— *Jock Macdonald: The Inner Landscape.* Toronto: Art Gallery of Ontario, 1985.

PERIODICALS:
Bates, Maxwell.
"Jock Macdonald, Painter – Explorer." *artscanada* 40th Anniversary Issue (March 1982): 79-81. Reprint of original: *Canadian Art* 14, no. 4 (1957).
Collinson, Helen.
"Lars Haukaness: Artist and Instructor." *Alberta History* 32, no. 4 (autumn, 1984): 11-20.
Davy, Ted G.
"Lawren Harris's Theosophic Philosophy." *The Canadian Theosophist* 72, no. 3 (1991).
Harris, Lawren.
"An Essay on Abstract Painting." *artscanada* 40th Anniversary Issue (March 1982): 39-43. Reprint of original: *Canadian Art* 6, no. 3 (1949).
Jackson, A.Y.
"Arthur Lismer – His Contribution to Canadian Art." *artscanada* 40th Anniversary Issue (March 1982): 50-51. Reprint of original: *Canadian Art* 7, no. 3 (1950).
Lismer, Arthur.
"Art and Life." *Foundations: Building the City of God*, 2nd series (Toronto: Student Christian Movement of Canada, 1927).

NEWSPAPERS AND PAMPHLETS:
"Art Scholarships said 'Useless,'" *The Albertan*, April 19, 1956.

"Exhibition and Sale of Paintings of the Canadian Rockies by Belmore Browne," The Casson Galleries, Boston, undated.
Gregory Horne,
Selected Climbing Routes of Mount Robson. Jasper: Gregory Horne Photographics, 1989.
— *Selected Climbing Routes of Mount Temple.* Jasper: Gregory Horne Photographics, 1990.
"Picture Exhibit at Museum Well Worth Visiting: Reminders Shown of Lars Haukaness," *Calgary Herald*, November 8, 1929.
Walter J. Phillips,
"Art and Artists," *Winnipeg Tribune*, August 26, 1933.
Walter J. Phillips,
"Sketching in Canada: Seasons: Winter," *Winnipeg Tribune*, April 15, 1939.
R.W. Sandford,
"Kathleen Daly Touches Everyone," *Banff Crag and Canyon*, June 3, 1987.
Nancy Tousley,
"Painter Found Spiritual Reality in the Arctic," *Calgary Herald*, June 21, 1991.
"Well Known Artist Dies in Rockies," *Calgary Herald*, September 6, 1929, night edition.
Suzanne Zwarun,
"Around the Town..." *Calgary Herald*, June 29, 1970.

MANUSCRIPTS AND OTHER SOURCES:
Archives of the Leighton Foundation, Millarville, Alberta:
A.C. Leighton papers.

Archives of the Whyte Museum of the Canadian Rockies, Banff, Alberta:
A.C. Leighton papers (M36).
Walter J. Phillips papers (M36).

Carl Rungius papers (M36).
Sound Tapes (S37/4, S37/21).
Mary Vaux papers (M36).
Catharine Whyte papers (M36).

CBC Radio broadcast,
Voice of the Pioneer, March-April, 1964.

Glenbow Museum Archives, Calgary, Alberta:
Canadian Art Galleries papers (M800, M8405).
Mabel Brinkley papers (M134).
Walter J. Phillips papers (M969).
Carl Rungius papers (M1084, M1085, M1086).

Glenbow Museum Library Artists Biographical Files (uncatalogued):
Charles Comfort
Lars Haukaness
Barbara Leighton

National Archives of Canada, Ottawa, Ontario:
Lawren S. Harris papers (30D 208, vol 2).
Arthur Lismer papers (30D 184, vol 3).
J.E.H. MacDonald papers (30D 111, vol 1-3).

INDEX

Titles of paintings are in *italics*; illustrations are in **bold**.

After September Snow
  (Belmore Browne): **22**
Agnes, Lake: **24**, 25
Alberta College of Art and Design:
  10, 15, 47
Amethyst Lake: **114**, 115
Assiniboine, Mount: **56-57**, 58, 59,
  60, 61, 63
Athabasca, Mount: **106**, 107

Banff, Alta.: 12, 15, 37, 39-40
Banff Centre for Continuing
  Education
  see Banff School of Fine Arts
Banff School of Fine Arts: 15
Barleigh
  see Leighton, Barbara
Beatty, J.W.: 10, 119
Beaver, Sampson: 110
Bell-Smith, Frederic Marlett: 23
  Morning, Lake Louise: **20**
Berg Glacier: **122**, 123
Berg Lake: 119, 123
Blue Glacier
  see Tumbling Glacier
Boulder Pass: **48**
Boulder Pass, Skoki
  (A.C. Leighton): **48**
Bow Lake: Dedication page, 100,
  104, 105
Bow Lake (Frederick Brigden):
  Dedication page, **104**, 105
Bow Valley Parkway: 17
Brachiopod, Mountain: **52**
Brachiopod Mountain
  (Carl Rungius): **52**
Brigden, Frederick: 105
  Bow Lake: Dedication page,
  104, 105
Browne, Belmore: 12, 19
  After September Snow: **22**
  Rainy Day at Marvel Lake: **62**
  Rising Clouds, Lake Louise: **18**
  Spring Reflections, Mount Rundle:
  11, 12

Canadian Group of Painters: 30
Canadian Pacific Railway
  artists: 2, 19, 23, 49

hotels, lodges, etc.: 19, 30, 59,
  67, 93
  role of: 2
Canmore, Alta.: 10, 30
Castle Mountain: **44**, 45
Cathedral Mountain: **70**, **84**, 85
Cathedral Mountain
  (Arthur Lismer): **84**
Cathedral Peak and Lake O'Hara
  (J.E.H. MacDonald): **70**
Chateau Lake Louise: 19
Clearing Weather, Sherbrooke Lake,
  Above Wapta Lake (J.E.H.
  MacDonald): **86**
colour: 10, 15, 17, 19, 25, 30, 32,
  34, 39, 51, 76
Columbia Icefield: 107
Comfort, Charles: 107, 115
  Mount Athabasca: **106**
  Ramparts, Amethyst Lake,
  Tonquin Valley, Jasper: **114**
Crowfoot Glacier: **98-99**, 100,
  101
Crowfoot Glacier (Carl Rungius):
  98-99, 100
Crowfoot Glacier (Catharine Robb
  Whyte): **101**
Crowfoot Mountain: **105**

Daly, Kathleen (Kay): 30
  Moraine Lake: **31**
Daly Glacier: 87
Daly, Mount: 87
des Poilus, Mont: 89-91

Eisenhower, Mount
  see Castle Mountain
Emerald Lake: 29, **92**, 93
Emerald Lake (Lawren Harris): 29,
  92, 93

Fairview, Mount: 40, **41**
Fay, Mount: *33*, 34
Floe Lake: **94-95**, 96
Floe Lake, Marble Canyon
  (A.C. Leighton): **94-95**, 96
Fripp, Thomas: 25, 40
  Lake in the Clouds, Lake Agnes: **24**
  Mount Fairview from Mount
  Temple: 40, **41**
From Larch Valley, Moraine Lake
  (Peter Whyte): **36**, 37

The Glacier (Arthur Lismer): **33**,
  34-35
glaciers: 18, 19, 22, 23, 33, 34, 88,
  90, **98-99**, 100, **101**, 106, 107,
  122, 123
Glaciers, Rocky Mountains (Lawren
  Harris): **88**, 90
Grassi, Lawrence: 76
Group of Seven: 4, 10, 35, 107
  see also names of individual
  members, e.g., Lismer, Arthur

Hammond, John:
  The Three Sisters: **2**, 3
Harris, Lawren: 4, 27, 29, 39-40,
  43, 69, 89, 93
  Emerald Lake: 29, **92**, 93
  Glaciers, Rocky Mountains: **88**, 90
  Isolation Peak, Rocky Mountains:
  90, **91**
  Maligne Lake: **108-109**
  Mount Lefroy: **28**
  Mount Robson: **116-117**
  Mount Sampson, Maligne Lake:
  112, 113
  Mount Temple: **42**, 43
  Tumbling Glacier, Berg Lake: **122**,
  123
Harvey, Barbara
  see Leighton, Barbara
Haukaness, Lars Jonson: 47
  Ptarmigan Pass, Canadian
  Rockies: **46**
hiking tips: 6
Huber, Mount: 85

Ice and Still Water, Canmore
  (Illingworth Kerr): **7-8**, 10
In the High Country, Wiwaxy Peak
  (Catharine Robb Whyte): **79**
Isolation Peak: 90, **91**
Isolation Peak, Rocky Mountains
  (Lawren Harris): 90, **91**

Jackson, A.Y.: 4, 119-120, **121**
  Mount Robson, Resplendent and
  Kain: **118**
Kain, Mount: **118**, 120
Kerr, Illingworth: 10
  Ice and Still Water, Canmore: **7-8**,
  10

Lake in the Clouds, Lake Agnes
  (Thomas Fripp): **24**, 25
Lake McArthur (Jock Macdonald):
  80, 81
Lake McArthur, Yoho Park (J.E.H.
  MacDonald): **83**
Lake O'Hara, September, 1916
  (John Singer Sargent): **64-65**, 67
Lake O'Hara with Snow (J.E.H.
  MacDonald): **74**, 76
lakes, glacial: 19, **24**, 25, 30, 32,
  94-95, 96
Larch Valley: **34**, 36
larches: 71, 96, 102, **103**
Lefroy Glacier: 19, 23
Lefroy, Mount: 19, 23, **28**, 29, **68**,
  75, 76
Leighton, A.C.: Opposite Table of
  Contents, 45, 49, 51, 59, 63, 97
  Boulder Pass, Skoki: **48**
  Floe Lake, Marble Canyon: **94-**
  95, 96
  Mount Assiniboine: **56-57**
  Mount Skoki: **50**, 51
Leighton, Barbara: 45, 49
  Mount Eisenhower: **44**, 45
  Mount Assiniboine: **58**
light: 10, 25
Lismer, Arthur: 4, 33-35, 85
  Cathedral Mountain: **84**
  The Glacier: **33**, 34-35
Louise, Lake: 18, 19, **20**, **21**, **22**

McArthur, Lake: **80**, 81, **83**
MacDonald, J.E.H.: Opposite
  Acknowledgements, 4, 71-73,
  74-76, 87
  Cathedral Peak and Lake O'Hara:
  70
  Clearing Weather, Sherbrooke
  Lake, Above Wapta Lake: **86**
  Lake McArthur, Yoho Park: **83**
  Lake O'Hara with Snow: **74**, 76
  Wiwaxy Peaks, Lake O'Hara: **72**
Macdonald, J.W.G. (Jock): 69, 81
  Lake McArthur: **80**
  Mount Lefroy, Lake O'Hara: **68**
Maligne Lake: **108-109**, 110
Maligne Lake (Lawren Harris):
  108-109
Marvel Lake: 62
The Mitre: 29

Moraine Lake: 30, **31**, 34, **36**
Moraine Lake (Kathleen Daly): 30,
31
Morning, Lake Louise (F.M. Bell-
Smith): 20, 23
Mount Assiniboine (A.C. Leighton):
56-57
Mount Assiniboine (Barbara
Leighton): 60
Mount Assiniboine, September Snow
(Peter Whyte): 58
Mount Athabasca (Charles
Comfort): 106, 107
Mount Eisenhower (Barbara
Leighton): 44, 45
Mount Lefroy (Lawren Harris): 28, 29
Mount Lefroy, Lake O'Hara (Jock
Macdonald): 68
Mount Robson (Lawren Harris):
116-117
*Mount Robson, Resplendent and
Kain* (A.Y. Jackson): **118**, 119
Mount Rundle, Banff (Walter J.
Phillips): **13**, 14-15
Mount Sampson, Maligne Lake
(Lawren Harris): **112**, 113
Mount Skoki (A.C. Leighton): **50**, 51
Mount Temple (Lawren Harris): **42**,
43
Mount Temple, Larches (Catharine
Robb Whyte): **103**
Mountain Lake (Carl Rungius): 77
Mountain Road (Walter J. Phillips):
16
mountains, on painting: 2, 14, 29,
35, 49, 55, 71, 85, 93, 119-120,
124

nationalism, artistic: 4, 30, 35, 87,
105
nature: 5, 15, 17, 35, 43, 81, 82
Niblock, Mount: 25
Niles, Mount: 87

Ogden, Mount: 87
O'Hara, Lake: Opposite
Acknowledgements, 14, 37,
64-65, 66-67, 70, 71, 73, 74, 76,
77, 78, 85
Ontario Society of Artists: 23
Opabin Plateau: 85

Paget Peak: 87
Paradise Valley: 34
Phillips, Walter J.: 14-15
Mount Rundle, Banff: **13**
Mountain Road: **16**
philosophy, artistic: 29, 69, 43, 69,
71, 81, 113
printmaking: 14-15, 45
Provincial Institute of Technology
and Art
see Alberta College of Art and
Design
Ptarmigan Pass: **46**, 47
Ptarmigan Pass, Canadian Rockies
(Lars Haukaness): **46**, 47
Ptarmigan, Peak: 53
Ptarmigan Peak (Carl Rungius): **53**

railways, role of: 2
Rainy Day at Marvel Lake (Belmore
Browne): **62**
*Ramparts, Amethyst Lake, Tonquin
Valley, Jasper* (Charles Comfort):
114, 115
The Ramparts: **114**, 115
Resplendent, Mount: **118**, 120,
121
Rising Clouds, Lake Louise
(Belmore Browne): **18**
Robb, Catharine
see Whyte, Catharine Robb
Robson, Mount: **116-117**, **118**,
119-120, 123
The Rockpile: 30
The Rockwall: 96
Romantic ideal: 2
Rundle, Mount: **11**, 12, **13**, 15
Rungius, Carl: 54-55
Brachiopod Mountain: **52**
Crowfoot Glacier: **98-99**, 100
Mountain Lake: **77**
Ptarmigan Peak: **53**

Samson, Mount: 110, **112**, 113
Sargent, John Singer: 67
Lake O'Hara, September, 1916:
64-65
Schäffer, Mary: 110
Sentinel Pass: 34, 35
Sherbrooke Lake: **86**, 87
Simpson, Jimmy: 54-55, 100, 105

Skoki, Mount: 50, 51
snow: 12, 17, 23, 40, 57, 59, 61, 65
Society of Canadian Artists: 23
Spring Reflections, Mount Rundle
(Belmore Browne): **11**, 12
Staples, Owen: **121**

Temple, Mount: 40, **42**, 43
Ten Peaks: 30, 34
theosophy: 29, 69
The Three Sisters: 2, 3, 7-8, 10
The Three Sisters (John
Hammond): 2, 3
Tonquin Valley: **114**, 115
Trail Riders of the Canadian
Rockies: 49, 55
Tumbling Glacier: **122**, 123
Tumbling Glacier, Berg Lake
(Lawren Harris): **122**

Valley of the Ten Peaks: 34, 39, 40
Vermilion Lakes: 12, 15
Victoria Glacier: 19, 23
Victoria, Mount: **75**, 76

Waterfall Valley: 89
weather: 12, 14-15, 37, 57, 59, 61,
65, 100, 120
Wenkchemna: 34
Whyte, Catharine Robb: 7, 37-39,
61, 73, 100
Crowfoot Glacier: **101**
*In the High Country, Wiwaxy
Peak*: **79**
Mount Temple, Larches: **103**
On the Rock Pile, Looking West:
38, 39
Whyte, Peter: 37, 39-40, 61, 73,
100
From Larch Valley, Moraine Lake:
36
*Mount Assiniboine, September
Snow*: **60**
Whyte Museum of the Canadian
Rockies: 37
Wiwaxy Peak: **72**, 79, 85
Wiwaxy Peaks, Lake O'Hara (J.E.H.
MacDonald): **72**

Yoho: 89

COLLECTORS:

Art Gallery of Hamilton, Hamilton,
    Ontario
The Edmonton Art Gallery,
    Edmonton, Alberta
Fogg Art Collection, Harvard
    University Art Museums,
    Cambridge, Massachusetts
Glenbow Museum, Calgary,
    Alberta
Don and Shirley Grace,
    Saanichton, British Columbia
Hart House Permanent Collection,
    University of Toronto, Toronto,
    Ontario
The Leighton Foundation,
    Millarville, Alberta
London Regional Art and
    Historical Museums, London,
    Ontario
McMichael Canadian Art
    Collection, Kleinburg, Ontario
Montreal Museum of Fine Arts,
    Montreal, Quebec
Morris and Helen Belkin Art
    Gallery, The University of
    British Columbia, Vancouver,
    British Columbia
National Gallery of Canada,
    Ottawa, Ontario
Whyte Museum of the Canadian
    Rockies, Banff, Alberta

PHOTOGRAPHY CREDITS:

Paintings
Rob Bos: The University of British
    Columbia, page 68
Anita Dammer: Glenbow,
    front and back cover (detail),
    frontispiece, pages 3, 8, 12, 13,
    16, 18, 20, 22, 24, 31, 41, 44,
    46, 48, 50, 52, 53, 60, 62, 74,
    77, 80, 95, 99, 104, 106, 112,
    114, 121, 122
Charles Hupé: National Gallery of
    Canada, pages 33, 83, 86
H. Korol: The Edmonton Art
    Gallery, page 56

All others courtesy of the collector,
photographer unknown.

Photographs
Courtesy of the Archives of the
Whyte Museum of the Canadian
Rockies, Banff, Alberta:

Byron Harmon:
    page 63 V727-NA66-2216
    page 97 V263/NA71-4291
Dan McGowan:
    front cover (inset)
    V408/NA86-122
    page 135 V408/NA-120
Peter and Catharine Whyte Fonds:
    page 7 V683/I.C.3
Photographer unknown:
    opposite Acknowledgements
    NA33-2253
Photographer unknown:
    opposite Table of Contents
    V727/16

Courtesy of Mrs. Margaret Knox,
Vancouver, British Columbia:
    page 27

David Christensen:
    Inside back flap

1. All references in this text are to Lawren Stewart Harris (1885 - 1970), and should not be confused with Lawren Phillips Harris (b.1910), the son of Lawren Stewart Harris, and also an accomplished painter.

2. The original members of the Group of Seven were: J.E.H. MacDonald (1873 - 1932), Lawren Harris (1885 - 1970), A.Y. Jackson (1882 - 1974), Arthur Lismer (1885 - 1969), Fred Varley (1881 - 1969), Frank Johnston (1888 - 1949), and Frank Carmichael (1890 - 1945). Johnston's association was brief and he left the Group in 1924, before he painted in the Rockies. Tom Thomson, always associated with the Group, died in 1917, before the Group had officially formed under that name.

3. Illingworth Kerr, *Paint and Circumstance* (Calgary: Jules and Maureen Poscente et al, 1987), 28.

4. Ibid., 28.

5. Ibid., 28.

6. Ibid., 107.

7. A.Y. Jackson was the only member of the original Group of Seven who painted on the prairies.

8. Roger Boulet, *The Tranquility and the Turbulence: The Life and Works of Walter J. Phillips* (Ontario: M.B. Loates Publishing, 1981), n.p.

9. Walter J. Phillips, "Sketching in Canada: Seasons: Winter," *The Winnipeg Evening Tribune*, 15 April 1939.

10. Maria Tippett and Douglas Cole, eds., *Phillips in Print: The Selected Writings of Walter J. Phillips on Canadian Nature and Art* (Winnipeg: The Manitoba Record Society, 1982), 54.

11. Ibid., 54.

12. Ibid., 28.

13. Ibid., 112.

14. Christopher Jackson, *North by West: The Arctic and Rocky Mountain Paintings of Lawren Harris, 1924 - 1931* (Calgary: Glenbow Museum, 1991), 21.

15. Arthur Lismer, "A.Y. Jackson, Painter of Canada, An Appreciation" (Lecture notes) Arthur Lismer papers, National Archives of Canada, 3: 19-20.

16. Peter Larisey, *Light for a Cold Land: Lawren Harris's Work and Life - An Interpretation* (Toronto: Dundurn Press, 1993), 100.

17. R.W. Sandford, "Kathleen Daly Touches Everyone," *Banff Crag and Canyon*, 3 June 1987.

18. *Voice of the Pioneer.* CBC Radio broadcast. March-April, 1964.

19. A.Y. Jackson, "Arthur Lismer - His Contribution to Canadian Art," *Canadian Art*, 7: no. 3 (spring, 1950), 50.

20. Ibid., 51.

21. Undelivered interview for CBC Radio, c.1964.

22. Arthur Lismer to J. Russell Harper, undated, as cited in Lois Darroch's *Bright Land: A Warm Look at Arthur Lismer* (Vancouver: Merritt Publishing Company, 1981), 69.

23. Ibid., 70.

24. Peter Whyte to Catharine Robb, Peter and Catharine Whyte papers, Whyte Museum of the Canadian Rockies (hereafter cited as Whyte papers), 20 December 1927.

25. Jon Whyte, *Mountain Glory: The Art of Peter and Catharine Whyte* (Banff: Whyte Museum of the Canadian Rockies, 1988), 25.

26. Lawren Harris to Catharine Robb Whyte, 4 April 1949, Whyte papers.

27. Suzanne Zwarun, "Around the Town...," *Calgary Herald*, 20 June 1970.

28. Ibid.

29. Haukaness wrote to W.G. Carpenter, who was then Head of the Institute, in 1927, stating: "my ambition [is] to make our art class at your school the Provincial Art School of Alberta..." Lars Haukaness to W.G. Carpenter, 17 May 1927, Lars Haukaness file, Glenbow Museum.

30. F.A. Key, (n.p., n.d.). See also: Collinson, "Lars Haukaness: Artist and Instructor," Lars Haukaness file, Glenbow Museum.

31. "Well Known Artist Dies in the Rockies," *Calgary Herald*, 6 July 1929, night edition.

32. Terry Fenton, *A.C. Leighton and the Canadian Rockies* (Banff: The Whyte Museum of the Canadian Rockies; Millarville: The Leighton Foundation, 1989), 17.

33. Two works were submitted to and accepted by the Academy, and shown in the December 1935 show. The other work depicts the Siwash Indian Village of Kakasilah, B.C. (not illustrated). Leighton was elected to the status of Associate Member of the Royal Canadian Academy that year.

34. The Leighton Residence and The Leighton Centre operate as The Leighton Foundation out of the studio home Leighton built near Millarville, Alberta. Artists' residence programs, children's art programs, and a rotating schedule of exhibitions are offered.

35. Walter J. Phillips, "Art and Artists," *Winnipeg Tribune*, 26 August 1933.

36. Personal notes, Carl Rungius papers, Glenbow Museum Archives, M1084.

37. Thanks to Brad White of Banff and Alex Edmund at Skoki Lodge, for information regarding the "rock palette" on Brachiopod Mountain.

38. Don Beers, *Banff - Assiniboine, Beautiful World* (Calgary: Highline Publishing, 1993), 39.

39. Mount Assiniboine journal notes, A.C. Leighton papers, Whyte Museum of the Canadian Rockies.

40. Ibid.

41. Ibid.

42. Catharine Robb Whyte to Edith Robb, 22 Sept. 1937, Whyte papers.

43. J.J. McArthur, Topographical survey of the Rocky Mountains, 1892.

44. John Singer Sargent to his cousin Mary, 30 August 1916, as quoted in Charles Merrill Mount, *John Singer Sargent, A Biography* (New York: W.W. Norton and Company, Inc., 1969), 334.

45. J.W.G. Macdonald, "Reflections on a Trip to the Canadian International Seminar in Breda," *Highlights* 4 March 1950, 6, as cited in Joyce Zemans's *Jock Macdonald* (Ottawa: National Gallery of Canada, 1985), 11.

46. J.W.G. Macdonald to John Varley, 9 September 1939, as cited in Joyce Zemans's *Jock Macdonald* (Ottawa: National Gallery of Canada, 1985), 17.

47. J.E.H. MacDonald diaries, National Archives of Canada (hereafter cited as MacDonald diaries) 30D 111, vol 1 file 1-11, August - September 1930.

48. MacDonald diaries, vol 1 file 1-12, September 1930.

49. In a 1927 letter to Catharine Robb, Peter Whyte states that he and MacDonald always seemed to be at O'Hara at the same time.

50. Peter Whyte to Catharine Robb, 12 September 1928, Whyte papers.

51. MacDonald diaries, vol 1 file 7, August - September 1930.

52. J.E.H. MacDonald to Peter Whyte, September 1930, Whyte papers.

53. J.E.H. MacDonald to Peter Whyte, 23 June 1931, Whyte papers.

54. Catharine Robb Whyte to Edith Robb, undated, Whyte papers.

55. Quoted in a letter from Thelma Van Alstyne to Joyce Zemans, as cited in Joyce Zemans's *Jock Macdonald* (Ottawa: National Gallery of Canada, 1985), 27.

56. Arthur Lismer in a letter to J. Russell Harper, undated, as cited in Lois Darroch's *Bright Land: A Warm Look at Arthur Lismer* (Vancouver: Merritt Publishing Company, 1981): 69-70.

57. J.E.H. MacDonald, "A Glimpse of the West," MacDonald papers, National Archives of Canada 30D 111 vol 3, file 36: 2-3.

58. Ibid., file 36: 6.

59. Graeme Pole, *Classic Hikes in the Canadian Rockies* (Canmore: Altitude Publishing Canada Ltd., 1994), 207.

60. As quoted in Bess Harris and R.G.P. Colgrove, *Lawren Harris* (Toronto: Macmillan of Canada, 1969), 62.

61. Terry Fenton, *A.C. Leighton and the Canadian Rockies* (Banff: Whyte Museum of the Canadian Rockies, 1989), 10.

62. The present version of Num-Ti-Jah Lodge includes expansions built in the 1930s, 40s, and 50s.

63. E.J. Hart, *Jimmy Simpson, Legend of the Rockies* (Canmore: Altitude Publishing Canada Ltd., 1991), 167.

64. Catharine Robb Whyte to Edith Robb, 8 August 1941, Whyte papers.

65. E.J. Hart, *Jimmy Simpson, Legend of the Rockies* (Canmore: Altitude Publishing Canada Ltd., 1991), 169.

66. A.Y. Jackson, *A Painter's Country: The Autobiography of A.Y. Jackson* (Toronto: Clarke, Irwin and Company Limited, 1958), 89.

67. E.J. Hart, *A Hunter of Peace* (Banff: Whyte Museum of the Canadian Rockies, 1980), 10.

68. Ibid., 80.

69. Ibid., 94.

70. Lawren Harris, *The Story of the Group of Seven* (Toronto: Rous and Mann Press Limited, 1964), 23.

71. A.Y. Jackson, *A Painter's Country: The Autobiography of A.Y. Jackson* (Toronto: Clarke, Irwin and Company Limited, 1958), 88.

72. Annie Besant and C.W. Leadbetter, *Thought-Forms* (Madras, 1957), as cited in Jeremy Adamson's *Lawren S. Harris: Urban Scenes and Wilderness Landscapes; 1906 - 1930* (Toronto: Art Gallery of Ontario, 1978), 179.

73. A.Y. Jackson, *A Painter's Country: The Autobiography of A.Y. Jackson* (Toronto: Clarke, Irwin and Company Limited, 1958), 31.

74. Ibid., 31.

75. Naomi Jackson Groves, *A.Y.'s Canada* (Vancouver: Clarke, Irwin and Company, Limited, 1968), 148.

76. Ibid., 150.

77. Ibid., 150.

78. Ibid., 150.

Carl Rugius painting on the Bow River, date unknown

SUGGESTED READING

For more information on trails and hiking in the Canadian Rockies:

Don Beers, *Banff – Assiniboine: A Beautiful World* (Calgary: Highline Publishing, 1993).

—. *Jasper – Robson: A Taste of Heaven* (Calgary: Highline Publishing, 1996).

—. *The Wonder of Yoho* (Calgary: Rocky Mountain Books, 1989).

—. *The World of Lake Louise* (Calgary: Highline Publishing, 1991).

Ben Gadd, *Handbook of the Canadian Rockies* (Jasper: Corax Press, 1995).

Brian Patton and Bart Robinson, *The Canadian Rockies Trail Guide* 6th edition (Canmore: Devil's Head Press, 1994).

Graeme Pole, *Classic Hikes in the Canadian Rockies* (Canmore: Altitude Publishing Canada Ltd., 1994).

For more information about the artists:

Charles C. Hill, *The Group of Seven: Art for a Nation* (Ottawa: The National Gallery of Canada; Ottawa: McClelland and Stewart, 1995).

Christopher Jackson, *North by West: The Arctic and Rocky Mountain Paintings of Lawren Harris, 1924 – 1931* (Calgary: Glenbow Museum, 1991).

Dennis Reid, *Our Own Country Canada* (Ottawa: National Gallery of Canada, 1979).